Child Abuse on the Internet

CHILD ABUSE ON THE INTERNET
Ending the Silence

Edited by
Carlos A. Arnaldo

Berghahn Books
New York • Oxford

UNESCO Publishing
PARIS

Published jointly by
the **United Nations Educational, Scientific and Cultural Organization**
The United Nations Educational, Scientific and Cultural Organization
7 place de Fontenoy, 75352 Paris 07 SP, France

and by
Berghahn Books
www.Berghahnbooks.com

Library of Congress Cataloging-in-Publication Data
Child abuse on the internet : breaking the silence / edited by Carlos A. Arnaldo
    p. cm.
    Includes index.
    ISBN 1-57181-245-8 -- ISBN 1-57181-246-6 (alk. paper)
    1. Child sexual abuse--Prevention. 2. Internet and children. 3. Children in
pornography--Prevention. I. Arnaldo, Carlos A.

HV6570.C545 2000
362.76--dc21   00-046742

British Library Cataloguing in Publication Data

A catalogue record for this book is available from the British Library.

Printed in the United States on acid-free paper.

ISBN UNESCO: 92-3-103728-5
ISBN Berghahn: 1-57181-245-8 hardback
ISBN Berghahn: 1-57181-246-6 paperback

*The designations employed and the presentation of material throughout this publication do not
imply the expression of any opinion whatsoever on the part of the UNESCO Secretariat concerning the legal status of any country, territory, city or area or of its authorities, or the delineation of
its frontiers or boundaries.*
*The authors are responsible for the choice and the presentation of the facts contained in this book
and for the opinions expressed therein, which are not necessarily those of UNESCO and do not
commit the Organization*

CONTENTS

ABBREVIATIONS

ACLU	American Civil Liberties Union
ACPE	Association Against Child Prostitution
AFA	Association of Internet Access Providers
AMADE	World Association of the Friends of Children
ANPPCAN	African Network for the Prevention and Protection against Child Abuse and Neglect
APEV	Association of Parents of Child Victims
CADEF	Action Committee for the Rights of Children and Women
CASPCAN	Cameroon Society for the Prevention of Child Abuse and Neglect
CEDECA	Centre for the Defence of Children's and Adolescents' Rights
CEJIL	Center for Justice and International Law
COFACE	Confederation of Family Organizations in the European Community
CRC	Convention on the Rights of the Child
CRCA	Children's Human Rights Centre of Albania
CRIDES	International Research and Documentation Centre on Sexual Exploitation
CRIN	Child Rights International Network
CSPCAN	Cameroon Society for Prevention of Child Abuse and Neglect
DCC	Direct Channel of Communication
EBU	European Broadcasting Union
EC/CE	European Commission/Commission EuropÇenne
ECPAT	End Child Prostitution, Child Pornography and Trafficking of Children for Sexual Purposes
EFCW	European Forum for Child Welfare
EMBRATUR	Brazilian Institute of Tourism
EuroIspa	European Association of Internet Service Providers

EU	European Union
FAQ	Frequently Asked Questions
FBI	Federal Bureau of Investigation
GRREM	Research Group on the Relation of Children and Media
ICEM	International Council of Educational Media
ICP	Internet Content Provider
IFJ	International Federation of Journalists
IGO	intergovernmental organization
IHAN	International Health Awareness Network
ILO	International Labour Organization
Interpol	International Criminal Police Organization
IRC	Internet relay chat
ISCA	International Save the Children Alliance
ISP	Internet Service Provider
ISPCAN	International Society for the Prevention of Child Abuse and Neglect
ITU	International Telecommunication Union
IWF	Internet Watch Foundation
MAPI	Movement Against Paedophilia on the Internet
MAPP	Movement to Abolish prostitution and Pornography
NGO	non-governmental organization
PEACE	Protecting Environment And Children Everywhere
PREDA	People's Recovery, Empowerment and Development Assistance Foundation
SOC-UM	Safeguarding our Children – United Mothers
UNAIDS	Joint United Nations Programme on HIV/Aids
UNCRC	The United Nations Convention on the Rights of the Child
UNESCO	United Nations Educational, Scientific and Cultural Organization
UNHCHR	United Nations High Commissioner's Office for Human Rights
UNICEF	United Nations International Children's Fund
WPFC	World Press Freedom Committee
WTO	World Tourism Organization

NOTES ON CONTRIBUTORS

Parry Aftab, Cyberspace lawyer, Head of the US Action Group to Protect Innocence in Danger.

Carol Aloysius, Associate editor and feature writer, *The Observer*, Sri Lanka.

Carlos A. Arnaldo, former Chief, Section for Communication Policies and Research, UNESCO, Paris.

Elisabeth Auclaire, President of the Commission on Children's Rights of the League of Human Rights, former President of the Groupe de Recherche sur la Relation Enfants/Médias and organizer of the international forum of researchers on 'Youth and the Media – Tomorrow' (UNESCO, Paris 21–25 April 1997).

Hélia Barbosa, Lawyer for Centre for the Defence of Children's and Adolescents' Rights (CEDECA) and End Child Prostitution, Child Pornography and Trafficking Children for Sexual Purpose (ECPAT) (Brazil).

Béatrice van Bastelaer, Movement Against Paedophilia on the Internet (MAPI), University of Notre Dame de la Paix, Namur, Belgium.

Ofelia Calcetas-Santos, United Nations Special Rapporteur on the Sale of Children, Child Prostitution and Child Pornography, practising lawyer for children's rights.

Ulla Carlsson, Coordinator of the UNESCO International Clearing House on Children and Violence on the Screen, University of Gothenburg, Sweden.

Rev. Fr Shay Cullen, President of People's Recovery, Empowerment and Development Assistance Foundation (PREDA), Olongapo, Philippines.

Pierre Dionne, Director-General, International Bureau for Children's Rights, Montreal.

Patrice Dunaigre, Paedo-psychiatrist and clinical psychoanalyst, Member of the Commission on Children's Rights of the League of Human Rights, France.

Agnès Fournier de Saint Maur, Specialized Crime Unit, Interpol General Secretariat, Lyon.

Gordon Fung, Assistant Commissioner of Police Crime, Hong Kong Police Headquarters.

Jo Groebel, Director-General of the European Institute for the Media (Dusseldorf) and Chair, Department of Media Competence, University of Utrecht; designed and implemented the UNESCO global research on young people's perception of violence on the screen in cooperation with the World Organization of the Scout Movement.

Bruce Harris, Executive Director, Latin American Programmes of Casa Alianza/Covenant House Latin America, Guatemala.

Mark Erik Hecht, Deputy Director of Human Rights Internet, a Canadian-based non-governmental organization specializing in human rights networking, documentation and publication; has completed research on 'The Internet and International Children's Rights', published as part of a textbook, *Human Rights on the Internet*.

Alex Corpus Hermoso, Director, People's Recovery, Empowerment and Development Assistance Foundation (PREDA), Olongapo, Philippines.

David Kerr, Chief Executive, Internet Watch Foundation, Cambridge.

Jean-Christophe Le Toquin, Permanent Delegate of the European Association of Internet Service Providers (EuroIspa).

Debbie Mahoney, Founder and Board President, Safeguarding our Children-United Mothers (SOC-UM), California.

Daniel Mbassa Menick, Prémontré Hospital Centre, France; Founder and Executive President, Cameroon Society for Prevention of Child Abuse and Neglect (CASPCAN).

Muireann O'Briain, Executive Director of ECPAT International (End Child Prostitution, Child Pornography and Trafficking of Children for Sexual Purposes), Bangkok; Senior Counsel of the Bar of Ireland, specializing in international human rights and children's rights law and commercial sexual exploitation of children.

Rachel O'Connell, Research Director, Cyberspace Research Unit, University of Central Lancashire; former Lecturer in the Department of Psychology, Leicester University, United Kingdom; Project Manager, the COPINE project, Department of Applied Psychology, University College, Cork, Ireland.

Philista Onyango, Director, African Network for the Prevention and Protection Against Child Abuse and Neglect (ANPPCAN), Nairobi, Kenya.

Aurela Pano, Executive Director, Children's Human Rights Centre of Albania.

Judge Andrée Ruffo, President of the International Bureau for Children's Rights, Montreal.

Helene Sackstein, Coordinator, Focal Point Programme against Sexual Exploitation of Children, NGO Group for the Convention on the Rights of the Child, Geneva.

Homayra Sellier, President, World Citizens' Movement to Protect Innocence in Danger; Founder and Director, White Lotus Foundation, Geneva.

Maureen Seneviratne, Chair of PEACE (Protecting Environment and Children Everywhere), Sri Lanka and of the National Group of ECPAT International; journalist and writer of children's books; appointed by Her Excellency, the President of Sri Lanka as a Member of the Board of the National Child Protection Authority of Sri Lanka and the National Monitoring Committee of the Convention on the Rights of the Child.

Kimberly Svevo, Executive Director, International Society for Prevention of Child Abuse and Neglect (ISPCAN), Chicago, United States.

Juanita Upadhyah, Special Projects Manager, International Society for Prevention of Child Abuse and Neglect (ISPCAN).

Aidan White, General Secretary, International Federation of Journalists, Brussels; Rapporteur of the Expert Meeting on Sexual Abuse of Children, Child Pornography and Paedophilia on the Internet; presented lead paper on the media at the 1996 Stockholm World Conference against Commercial Sexual Exploitation of Children.

PREFACE

The International community has now begun to mobilize against the scourge of paedophilia on the Internet. UNESCO has sought to fulfil its ethical mission by helping to break the silence on this perverse and pernicious abuse of the most fundamental rights of the child. In calling the 'Expert Meeting on Sexual Abuse of Children, Child Pornography and Paedophilia on the Internet: an International Challenge' at its Headquarters in Paris in January 1999, UNESCO sought to provide a forum for United Nations specialized agencies, governmental and non-governmental organizations, foundations, the police and judiciary, educators, psychologists and the media to assess the role and contribution of all actors in the fight against child pornography and paedophilia on the Internet.

The international dimension of the effort to end child abuse on the Internet is an essential one. When crime is not restricted by national borders and its perpetrators deliberately exploit a frontier-free medium to further their ends, a global counter-offensive is required. This is why the UNESCO Meeting adopted a Plan of Action as a framework for a coordinated international response.

It is hoped that this publication will not only fulfil the vital function of providing up-to-date information, but that it will also enable us, in partnership, to evaluate and coordinate the world-wide efforts underway to combat the sexual abuse of children through the misuse of the freedom of communication that the Internet offers.

INTRODUCTION

Children have been subjected to violence – physical, psychological and sexual – since the dawn of humankind. Slaughter, enslavement and rape of children have attended war and conflict from pre-history to today's newspaper. Abraham was prepared to murder his child to honour his deity. Generations of first-born babies were killed for reasons of religious or political expediency. Children have been made to labour in the fields, among the flocks and herds, and in the factories in virtually all societies at one time or another. Throughout history and in different social and cultural contexts, female children have been considered as something less than human – neglected, abandoned, killed, sexually maimed and mistreated. How many barely adolescent girls – and boys – have practised the world's oldest profession, willingly or otherwise, over the millennia?

Only in the latter half of the twentieth century did the world community formally decide of a common accord that children have rights and that violence of any kind against them constitutes abuse and an unacceptable infringement of those rights. Having adopted the Universal Declaration of Human Rights and the United Nations Convention on the Rights of the Child, the international community has increasingly sought to find the means to protect children from abuse, to eliminate the root causes of abuse, to apprehend and heal the abuser, and to rehabilitate and reintegrate abused children so that they can live normal lives.

Sexual abuse of children in particular remains pervasive. This form of violence against children has, until very recently, remained cloaked in a silence imposed by cultural and social mores and taboos, by fear, shame and ignorance, and by the absence of a concerted and coherent response to the problem on the part of modern civil societies.

The media are to be credited for having contributed most over the last two decades of the twentieth century to confronting us, wherever we live on the planet, with the risks and the reality of sexual violence against our children. Paedophilia, child pornography, sex tourism, the no-win equation of sex-for-money-for-drugs – itself an indefatigable syndrome – as well as the destructive sociology of poverty, war, social and family breakdown in league with the attractive economics of trafficking in children for prostitution. The bottom line is that we can no longer say we do not know.

The Internet, a medium of a new and different sort, has added a late-twentieth century twist, a new 'virtual' variable to the problem of sexual abuse of children, specifically as regards pornography and paedophilia. This was the focus of the 'Expert Meeting on Sexual Abuse of Children, Child Pornography and Paedophilia on the Internet: An International Challenge' which was held at the initiative of UNESCO's Director-General on 18 and 19 January 1999 at UNESCO Headquarters in Paris and which is the subject of this work.

This volume is organized thematically, based on the submissions and interventions of the participants, as well as on a limited amount of other relevant material made available to the UNESCO Secretariat.

Part One begins with the overall context of sexual abuse of children in the world today, then attempts to define precisely what is understood in sociological, psychological and legal terms by child pornography and paedophilia. The phenomena of child pornography and paedophilia on the Internet are then considered in detail.

Part Two considers the strategies that are being – or could be – adopted to combat these problems. These may be legal and regulatory approaches imposed by governments; policies of self-regulation by the Internet industry; and action by individuals, parents, civic groups and NGOs or, as is in fact the case, a combination of all of these. As will be apparent on reading, the debate about just what is the appropriate combination is a lively one. The need for further research is underlined.

Part Three presents the Declaration and Plan of Action adopted by the participants at the UNESCO Meeting, as well as information on follow-up activities already undertaken or planned. Annexes contain information of a practical nature such as the text of the UN convention on the rights of the child, lists of relevant Internet websites and discussion groups, and references.

If the media in most countries have confronted us with the reality and extent of paedophilia and child pornography, the Internet, by its very nature, has brought these phenomena into our homes. Should we wish – and most of us do not – we can now see it for ourselves. And so can our children. Virtual pornography, virtual flashing and virtual soliciting for pornographic ends or sex are but a keystroke away. And once caught in this mire, it is sometimes difficult to get out.

To survive and thrive 'commercially', child pornography and paedophilia were long constrained by the need for physical proximity (family and friends, neighbourhood, community and town) and physical communication supports (magazines, photographs, films and videos). Almost universally proscribed by law and/or by social and cultural taboos, these phenomena were hidden and secret – more rarely relegated to 'red light districts' under close police surveillance – but subject nonetheless to severe repression when revealed. Low-cost air travel has removed the proximity constraint. The Internet and other interactive electronic networks are in the process of removing the communication restraint.

The Internet in particular, with its growing capacity to exchange in real time written messages, telephone calls, data, sound, still and moving pictures, has broken the traditional communication barriers and makes incalculable quantities of information of all kinds and all forms instantly available to anyone with a personal computer – at any time and place in the world. Most Internet users seek social or professional contact and conversation, entertainment and information. Most Internet content providers and millions of existing individual websites cater to this demand – and in a way that causes problems only for the national and international telecommunications regulators left behind in the dust, and the large national and multinational carriers that have traditionally dominated and controlled international electronic communications.

However, several hundred thousand commercial and private websites – proliferating daily – cater to that most basic of all instincts, sex. This is more or less acceptable depending on the social, cultural and legal context of the provider and user. A smaller but apparently growing number of Internet websites, FTP databases, newsgroups and chat rooms are devoted to sexual perversion, child pornography and paedophilia. This is not acceptable, anywhere.

The question is, what should be done?

PART ONE

THE PROBLEM AND ITS CONTEXT

Real World and Cyberworld: Sexual Abuse of Children Today

Child pornography and paedophilia on the Internet are not stand-alone phenomena that have appeared *ex nihilo*. They are merely the extension using the most modern means – the new field of action offered by the Internet – of historical and present- day forms of sexual abuse of children. They fit into a larger context of ongoing child abuse about which one can read almost any day and in almost any newspaper and with which humankind has yet to come to terms, let alone contain.

UNESCO's 'Expert Meeting on Sexual Abuse of Children, Child Pornography and Paedophilia on the Internet: An International Challenge' began by considering the broad issue of sexual abuse of children today as it is found almost everywhere around the globe. If the Internet and its applications, good and bad, remain confined largely to the so-called 'developed world' today, there is little doubt that 'the Net' will expand rapidly into the 'developing world', if not tomorrow, then very soon. And in the realm of sexual abuse of children, it will simply provide one more means to the child abusers and exploiters, the pimps, procurers, pornographers and paedophiles who are already there today.

This section shows to just what extent such people are already – and increasingly – active. Following a global overview of child abuse and neglect, and succinct regional reviews, a number of individual country reports are presented.

Chapter 1

A GLOBAL OVERVIEW OF CHILD ABUSE AND NEGLECT

Kimberly Svevo

The vulnerability of children, from infancy throughout their childhood years of dependency on adults for safety and nurturing, puts them at risk of neglect and maltreatment in many forms. Extreme forms of maltreatment – including child soldiering, child prostitution, child physical abuse, child sexual abuse and – child labour – are generally abhorred, and attempts are made to prevent such extreme abuse in most countries. Yet professionals are reluctant to even estimate the number of the world's children suffering from some sort of abuse. One of the major obstacles to understanding the scope of the problem is the fact that only a very small number of respondents are able to provide substantiated data regarding the number of children reported as abused. Further, definitions of abuse are not yet consistent within some countries, much less from country to country or region to region. Yet professionals do estimate that the number of abused and neglected children is at an emergency level, since there is a tragic lack of protection available to children at risk world-wide.

The visible and invisible scars of past child abuse prevent many people from achieving their potential, thereby draining our global society of much good – while fomenting a spirit of mistrust, anger and hatred which impacts each of our lives. International research indicates that the potential for maltreatment exists in all social strata and very many families at some point in a child's development, as David Finkelhor reports in the 1996 Report of the International Society for Prevention of Child Abuse and Neglect (ISPCAN).

Child abuse awareness and prevention activities continue in an upward trend, revealing many exciting developments and possibilities. Perhaps most importantly, our knowledge base about the problem is expanding at a rapid rate. Journals are filled with reports about new treatment approaches and insights about the causes and consequences of abuse. The foundation of the professional expertise grows broader and stronger every year. More and more practitioners from different disciplinary backgrounds have been trained and developed specialisation in the field. And this knowledge and awareness is expanding across international boundaries at a rapid pace. Every year new places in the world add concern about child abuse to their social and political agendas, including places that at one time seemed very remote from the discussion of these issues. International awareness is also reflected in new involvement by international organizations in the cause.

At the same time, however, there are alarming developments in the global and historical picture of the child abuse problem. On every front, one can find social, economic and even technological forces that have clearly aggravating effects on the well-being of children. These range from the growing divorce rate, the expansion of armed conflicts in various places around the world, to the environmental degradation that disrupts social and cultural balances. Governmental commitment to remedy the problem of child abuse seems weak, non-existent or flagging in many places. And there is also, in many locales, an increasing organized opposition to some of the goals sought by child abuse advocates.

Although it is often stated that children are the world's most valuable resources, our 'future' children's rights are – even today and throughout the world – largely ignored, often leading to a tragic outcome. In this area, the United Nations Convention on the Rights of the Child provides an important foundation for significant work to be done to guarantee children's rights globally.

Certain child abuse and neglect issues are common in almost all countries, including physical, sexual, emotional and psychological abuse, abandonment and, increasingly, problems of street children (*World Perspectives*, 1998). There are also many issues which are more prevalent in certain regions of the world. For instance, figures for child labour and child sexual exploitation are especially high in Asia in view of high population density, severe economic problems, scant education and a culture of strict discipline of children. Wars and government instability in countries in Eastern Europe, Africa and Latin America are also creating major problems with child soldiers, refugee children, children confined to institutions and other issues specific to child victims of war. Central America and Asia, suffering from frequent natural disasters, showed a tremendous increase in 1998 alone in the number of homeless children and street children.

Child abuse and neglect prevention is still a new field, and many approaches and methods of treatment remain controversial. The lack of international data on the incidence of child abuse and methods of addressing treatment and prevention is currently motivating ISPCAN to devote significant effort to this area. ISPCAN is currently involved with efforts to both increase data collection and related research, as well as to identify 'best practice models' and develop guidelines to assist child abuse and neglect prevention professionals and policy-makers world-wide.

The next section of this chapter provides an overview of key child abuse and neglect issues and efforts from regional perspectives. While geographic and resource availability issues have a strong impact on the key issues and approaches to child abuse and neglect prevention in different countries, so also do the issues of level of education, rate of urbanization and cultural approaches to human rights in general.

A brief glance at child abuse and neglect in North America

Deborah Daro and Kimberly Svevo

Each year, one million children in North America are confirmed as victims of child abuse or neglect and over 1,200 die as a result of parental mistreatment. Overall, the reported rate of child abuse has increased by more than 300 per cent since 1976. Both public and private responses to this issue have expanded with the growing number of reports, as evidenced by increased public child welfare budgets and the widespread availability of various child abuse prevention services in most United States communities. 'There can be no more delusions – no-one can deny that the problem of children being sold for sex exists, here and now, in almost every country in the world,' Professor Viti Muntarbhorn, former UN Special Rapporteur on The Sale of Children, Child Prostitution and Child Pornography.

Many people in both the public and private sectors have lost faith in the current child welfare system to accurately identify and assist victims of maltreatment. Several distinct trends deserve mention here:

- The number of child abuse reports continue to climb, suggesting that the scope of the problem, from a public policy perspective, is not diminishing. In 1994, over 3.1 million reports of child abuse were received by local child protective service agencies;
- Increasingly, children being referred to child protective services come from seriously troubled and chaotic family situations. Paternal substance abuse, violent and abusive partners, and multiple environmental and personal risk factors make it increasingly difficult for child welfare agencies to ensure the safety of a child remaining in its home;
- On the other hand, parenting practices with respect to the use of corporal punishment and other negative methods of disciplining children appear to be on the decline, suggesting prevention efforts are having an impact.

Current strategies and efforts of organizations involved in assisting with child abuse, neglect and protection focus on providing education, training, research and practical information and materials to professionals working with children, families, as well associal policies. In addition, increased efforts are being made to support and inform first-time parents, at-risk families – and children – regarding good parenting. The legal system is increasingly aware of children's rights, but the balance between children's and parents' rights is often still controversial.

'States Parties shall ensure that the institutions, services and facilities responsible for the care or protection of children shall conform with the standards established by competent authorities, particularly in the areas of safety, health, in the number and suitability of their staff, as well as competent supervision.' Article 3, United Nations Convention on the Rights of the Child.

Successful Approaches Needed in the Future

As with all countries world-wide, those in North America require a critical evaluation of current systems and policies, better information on successful models of what is working to prevent child abuse and neglect elsewhere in the world, and a serious investment by all governments to: improve systems, policies and resources for child abuse and neglect prevention (including treatment of children, families and perpetrators); more rigorously measure key constructs of interest such as parental capacity, social supports, parent-child interaction, among others; better recognize and incorporate conflicting evaluation results into the planning process; establish a national data system for documenting the scope of the child abuse problem and public investment in interventions to address this issue; make these resources and systems available and responsive to all in need; change attitudes from punitive to therapeutic (with long-term goals of rehabilitation); and increase the quality of child abuse and neglect prevention training for all professionals working with children and families.

A brief glance at child abuse and neglect in the Asian Region

Juanita Upadhyay

The largest population of children in the world live in Asia and yet the majority of these are subject to a lack of access to proper medical health care, nutrition, education and social conditions. This reflects the socioeconomic reality of the developing countries of Asia. The main factors that contribute to the magnitude of the problem are poverty, illiteracy, tradition and superstition, caste systems, landlessness, lack of economic opportunities, rural-urban migration, population growth, political instability and the weak implementation of legal provisions. International standards and conventions have paved the way for a slow change in realization of basic human rights in the Asian countries.

Major child abuse and neglect issues in Asia requiring a strong focus and currently being addressed include: slavery/bonded labour; child soldiers (in Cambodia and Myanmar); child pornography; abandoned children living in the streets; exposure to violence; environmental hazards – extreme hot and cold working conditions (in welding, glass-blowing factories, deep-sea fishing, etc.), exposure to dangerous chemicals, pollution, etc.; child marriage (especially in South Asian countries such as India, Nepal and Bangladesh); child labour (child domestic workers, factory workers, prostitutes, porters); female infanticide; trafficking of children for commercial exploitation (prostitution, begging, organ trade); malnutrition, and children with HIV, Aids and other illnesses.

Cultural advantages and disadvantages which affect the risk of child abuse and neglect positively or negatively include: early marriage; caste systems in India and Nepal – lower caste populations are the most disadvantaged and marginalized; discrimination against female children (malnutrition, deprivation of medical benefits, education, etc.); agriculture-based economies which compel families to force children from an early age to work in the fields, in the household and also as wage labourers; ethnic cultural practices which tolerate early marriage, polygamy, drinking and prostitution both in South Asia and South East Asia; religious practices such as offering female children to God as Devdasis in Nepal and India and who in reality perform as sex slaves; illiteracy, tradition and superstition which inhibit families from accessing health, education and other basic rights; and migration from rural to urban areas which leads to breakdown of families, landlessness, street children, trafficking of children, etc.

Successful approaches for the future

Among the approaches to combat the issues in the future are: the establishment of a reliable and standardized information collection process; awareness-raising campaigns in rural and urban areas among community leaders, teachers, police, social workers, parents and children themselves; the need to increase know-how (in detection, assessment, reporting, treatment and prevention) of multidisciplinary professionals (police, lawyers, doctors, judges, social workers, teachers, etc.) working with child abuse and neglect (in many instances, child victims even when rescued have suffered further due to the lack of proper medical facilities for treatment and rehabilitation); and cooperation between governmental and non-governmental organizations, people's organizations, the agencies of the United Nations system and other international organizations in developing concerted actions.

A review of child abuse and neglect in Africa

Daniel Mbassa Menick

Major child abuse and neglect issues in Africa requiring a strong focus, and currently being addressed, include street children (abandonment), physical abuse, sexual abuse and child labour.

Related issues which need urgently to be addressed include:

- Children and armed conflict: wars are the most important context for the abuse of children. Millions of children are victims of war, massacred, wounded, tortured, starved or recruited as soldiers and exposed to horrific experiences. Africa has been the continent where the use of child soldiers has been the most prevalent;
- Children and HIV/Aids: many children are abandoned, rejected or become orphans as a result of having parents with HIV/Aids, not counting those actually suffering themselves from the disease;
- Child prostitution: this is spreading in Africa (for example in Dakar and Nairobi);
- Female genital mutilation which maims and often kills;
- Child abduction for sale (in Mauritania and Benin, for instance).

Cultural advantages and disadvantages which impact the risk of child abuse and neglect positively or negatively include: early marriage; persistence of male domination; female genital mutilation; strict cultural rules binding children to obey adults; acceptance of physical abuse as a disciplinary method in the community; the need to support economically extended family systems, which are under pressure from trends toward urbanization: family systems in jeopardy promote tolerance of new and degrading forms of behaviour, joint liability, partition (sharing) of properties, etc.

Major regional challenges include: gathering information and data; addressing sensitive issues and implementing difficult solutions; overcoming the taboo of speaking about child abuse issues, especially sexual abuse; changing perceptions that child physical abuse is an accepted disciplinary method in the community; and lack of trained researchers to address the issue and funds to pay the researchers.

Successful approaches for the future

The lack of commitment and involvement of national governments in defining policies on these issues is a big problem for the NGOs. Where legislation exists on child protection issues, the laws are not always respected and courts of law rarely deal severely with those not in conformance. The most critical factor today is generating support for NGOs by the local governments.

Intensive sensitization efforts will achieve positive effects. The training of professionals will also develop increased interest in child abuse and neglect prevention, and will ultimately facilitate good data collection. It is also important to encourage the involvement of those in community justice, as they have an important role to play in designing and enforcing child protection policy.

An overview of child abuse and neglect in the European region

Juanita Upadhyay

Among the declining population of children in the European Union countries, it is estimated that 600,000 children are abused every year. Surveys carried out in different European countries (France, Italy, United Kingdom) reveal that five out of every 1,000 children each year experience serious maltreatment and have to be taken into care by the authorities (WHO).

In Central and Eastern European countries, political and economic changes in the 1990s uncovered and created a variety of situations in which children are particularly vulnerable. Such situations include children in institutions, on the streets, in conflict with the law or quite simply as victims of severe poverty whilst remaining in their own families and communities. In these countries it is estimated by WHO that 30 out of every 1,000 children – six times more than in EU countries – are abused and even more in cases of the most extreme socio-economic conditions.

Major child abuse and neglect issues in Europe requiring a strong focus, and currently being addressed include: children of war; refugee children; street children; malnourished children; children and HIV/Aids; children in conflict with law; disability; abandonment; and child mortality.

Cultural disadvantages affecting the risk of child abuse and neglect include: the decreasing proportion of children in the overall population; breakdown of families and the increased incidence of single parent families; multiracial societies; cultural, religious and traditional influences of criminalizing child abuse rather than treating it; poverty; war and migration.

Organizations currently involved in assisting with child abuse and neglect prevention include: the Co-federation of Family Organization in the European Communities (COFACE) which speaks up for families and organizes contacts and exchanges of ideas and experiences in various countries; the European Forum for Child Welfare (EFCW) which monitors and influences legislation and development of policies affecting children, and modifies the criteria by which European Union funds are distributed and secured for children to ensure a fair allocation of resources. Numerous non-governmental organizations are involved in: providing opportunities for training and capacity-building of professionals working with children;

gathering and dissemination of information on best practices; and other efforts in prevention.

ISPCAN overview and potential

The International Society for Prevention of Child Abuse and Neglect (ISPCAN), founded by Henry Kempe in 1977, is a unique multidisciplinary non-governmental organization working to prevent child abuse and neglect around the world. The aim of ISPCAN is to prevent cruelty to children, whether it is inside or outside the family.

ISPCAN is committed to developing educational training and cooperative efforts to prevent such violence, to increase awareness of all forms of child maltreatment, and to promote the rights of children in every nation, in every form. The Society works in Cupertino with fellow child- and health-focused organizations, national and municipal governments, and funding agencies to provide: education (congresses, regional conferences, national and local training seminars); research; publications (journals, newsletters, membership directories, books of abstracts and special reports) and sustainable child abuse and neglect prevention societies of multidisciplinary professionals in child protection active on regional and country levels.

Invitation to Joint Action to Prevent Child Abuse and Neglect

ISPCAN invited UNESCO and NGOs present at the January 1999 Meeting to consider partnerships to bring child abuse and neglect training, education, information, resources and collaborative opportunities to countries throughout the world. As part of ISPCAN's commitment to building the required professional and technical capacity throughout the world, it also invited involvement in: a coordinated effort to collect accurate information on national incidence of child abuse world-wide, based on common definitions of abuse; identifying which child abuse and neglect prevention organizations and efforts, and governmental/legal systems/policies, exist and where (through local professionals) and evaluating their strengths, weaknesses and potential; and shouldering these existing cores of committed professionals working to prevent child abuse and neglect, while bringing them together to establish sustainable organizations of concerned professionals as multidisciplinary child abuse and neglect associations and to organize child protection efforts in local communities as well as on a national and regional basis.

Together, we may be able to more effectively: identify and engage professionals and organizations that can help champion efforts to prevent child abuse and neglect in their countries and regions, and build teams for sustainable efforts; build increased awareness of the issues of child abuse and neglect within the public and thence with policy-makers; generate a movement to establish increased training and education for professionals and the public (including children); organize technical resources/materials, guidelines and best practices, as well as mentors and trainers who can help effect change within social infrastructures and policies, as well as through all organizations – law enforcement, hospitals, schools, social/welfare agencies, institutions, legal systems and governments, and collaborate in an effort to attract financial resources for the eradication of child abuse and neglect, and the treatment of abused children and their families.

Chapter 2

Sri Lanka: protecting environment and children everywhere

Maureen Seneviratne

Introduction

'In five ways should parents show their love for their child: by restraining him from vice, by exhorting him to virtue, by training him in a profession, by contracting a suitable marriage for him and in due time handing over to him his inheritance', so says the Sigalovada Suttanta Discourse of the Buddha. For thousands of years children in Sri Lanka have been regarded as a treasure (*vasthuwa*), not only embellishing the worth and prestige of their families and their parents, but also of society as a whole.

Nonetheless, history shows that child abuse has always existed, even if it remains very much an invisible problem. Child abuse within families both in villages and in towns has been and remains quite common, although studies and reporting on it have been insignificant. It is even taken for granted in some communities, but not openly alluded to. Child activists come up against considerable obstacles when attempting to bring offenders to justice or even to counsel them or arrange psychiatric treatment. A girl who became pregnant as a result of abuse within her family would usually be aborted according to traditional medical means known to almost all village folk. If this failed, the child would be born and brought up quite normally within the family circle. However, boys sexually harassed and maltreated would often undergo severe trauma.

Although the phenomenon of 'sex tourism' – involving mainly men travelling to other countries to engage in sex with children – is well documented, commercial sexual exploitation of children is predominantly a local issue, with both clients and agents coming from the local community.' World Congress on the Commercial Sexual Exploitation of Children: Overview.

Commercial sexual exploitation, however, is a phenomenon that manifested itself in the late 1950s with the advent of 'sex tourism' by foreigners addicted to sex with young boys (14 to 18 years old) and who, at that time, could 'buy' a boy for as little as two rupees (a few US cents). These foreigners came to Sri Lanka on tourist or business visas, stayed on for long periods and kept returning year after year. Very soon they had their own houses, offices and business interests in Sri Lanka and retinues of young boys to abuse (the modern bonded slaves). Child sexual abuse and incest were not discussed openly for the simple reason that these topics were considered 'dirty' and 'indecent' for public discourse. They were also mistakenly believed not to exist in Sri Lanka or simply swept under the carpet. But during the 1980s and 1990s, child sexual abuse has been publicly recognized as a very serious problem.

With the government actively sponsoring tourism in the 1970s and 1980s, and the construction of a large number of five-star hotels in beach areas, hundreds of thousands of tourists from all over the globe visited Sri Lanka and tourism became the key foreign exchange earner for the country. We regard 1980 as a watershed for the shattering of some preconceived notions that tourism could be 'contained' and 'prevented' from affecting the social culture of the country. The report on child prostitution by Tim Bond of *Terre des Hommes* revealed that:

> Sri Lanka was becoming well known among certain circles in Europe as an easy and cheap source of young boys for sex and that paedophiles from all parts of the world came each year to Sri Lanka to satisfy their sexual preferences for children, and having visited once the country, came back again and again.

The government of Sri Lanka took immediate action by studying legislation to prohibit and prevent the commercial sexual exploitation of children. Several other reports commissioned thereafter by the government revealed the shocking reality that children, mainly boys, as young as ten years of age, were being sexually exploited by paedophiles entering the country with tourist visas and illegally over-staying the permitted period. Relevant draft legislation was presented to the Cabinet for approval in August 1987. The Minister of State (under whose purview was tourism) decided that there was 'no necessity' to adopt a new law curbing commercial sexual exploitation of children.

By 1984, Sri Lanka was already caught in the throes of a violent ethnic conflict between Tamil opposition groups in the north and the east demanding a separate state and government security forces fighting to preserve the unity, territorial integrity and sovereignty of Sri Lanka. With the intervention of the Indian Army in 1997, tourism reached a low ebb. By 1988, research conducted by concerned groups such as Protecting Environment and Children Everywhere (PEACE) showed that if conventional tourism had been reduced to a dribble because of the adverse sociopolitical situation in Sri Lanka, a certain brand and breed of 'visitor' was still boldly entering the country, putting up in small innocuous guesthouses, rooms and apartments in residential areas and tourist complexes. This 'visitor' was there all the year round, sexually exploiting young boys with impunity. The demand for younger and younger boys by paedophiles is today all too evident. Old myths are far from forgotten: since ancient times it has been believed that sex with prepubescent girls or boys can cure adults of venereal diseases – and nowadays of Aids – or at least prevent their transmission as the young children are 'clean'. And if paedophiles constitute only a minimal percentage of the tourist influx today, the damage they do to hundreds, not to say thousands, of children is grave, destructive and often permanent.

Profiles of child victims

Our research during the 1990s and our experience gathered through the work we do as part of the Global Campaign: End Child Prostitution, Pornography and Trafficking of Children shows that there are two types of children in prostitution.

Our case studies suggest that 'beach boys', i.e., boy prostitutes, are mostly self-employed and either work alone or in gangs (though it does happen that a small hotel or guesthouse owner may run a brothel for boys). These self-employed boys, ranging in age from 8 to 15, ply their trade in the beach resort areas along the west and south-west coasts. They are usually school dropouts, lured into prostitution by the prospect of quick and easy money but in fact working for tiny financial rewards. A large number of these beach boys are drawn from fishing hamlets or coastal villages and many are extremely poor. About 30 per cent of them, however, are from villages in the hinterland – some from reasonably stable homes with a middle-class background – and are lured to the beach not because of their poverty but because of 'golden dreams' promised by agents who slip into the villages to recruit them. The 'dream' in this instance is the prospect of 'adoption' by foreign visitors who might take the children away to Australia, Europe or North America. The fact that only one percent get such an opportunity is unheeded because abused boys rarely return to their homes. Most of these child victims eagerly look forward to the ultimate goal of travelling abroad as the favoured playmate of the paedophile. The possibility of being discarded by their paedophile partners as they grow older, then to confront a future without prospects, seems to these children an unreal and distant eventuality.

More perturbing and far more difficult to investigate is the problem of bonded children, those who have been used in prostitution and pornography for more than five years and who are controlled by large international rings. They exist in the beach areas from where they are moved into many parts of the country by their agents, yet this traffic is rarely discussed in Sri Lankan society. Most of these child victims come from the poorest homes in the tourist areas. Significant numbers are brought into these areas from the hinterland by agents and pimps. They are brought from the rural areas by the prospect of employment but are lured into prostitution by unscrupulous agents.

> Child exploitation must be fought in tourism but we must not confuse tourism with what is one of its main perversions. Francisco Frangialli, Executive Director, World Tourism Organization.

These children are virtual prisoners and are kept in houses near the resort areas. Some are confined in what are termed orphanages that arerun by local people with foreign assistance. We know where some of them are sited, who controls them and who is involved, but have been unable to take action because these people are supported by powerful persons in Sri Lanka and by international networks. However, we try to constantly monitor and lobby against them, and in a few instances have been successful in bringing the culprits, both local and foreign, to book. Young children used in this manner, discarded after a season or two, are quite unable to keep a lasting relationship with their abusers. They are doomed to a life of crime thereafter.

According to police investigations and claims of social workers, they usually end up as drug addicts or alcoholics and, unless removed from corrupting influences at an early date, are almost impossible to rehabilitate. Very little is understood, even by social workers, in the country about the psychological trauma these children endure by being sexually exploited.

In Sri Lanka, being an island, cross-border trafficking of children for sexual purposes is not a problem. But there is 'in-country' trafficking of children from the rural areas to the city and tourist complex areas, organized by gangs of agents or pimps, master-minded by powerful thugs, sometimes with the connivance and blessings of authoritative circles. Nothing very much can be done to break up and break through these rings due to their connections with those in power.

Another phenomenon leading to commercial sexual abuse of children occurs when children peddle wares on the beach. Children are accustomed to selling fruits, batiks and so forth. When they meet foreigners the children may receive gifts or money, they become friendly and the opportunity is created for sexual abuse. The children walk on the beach trying to obtain gifts and meet tourist guides (agents) acting as intermediaries to procure children. Some of these children have sexual relations with foreigners after having been introduced by agents or pimps. Hence sexual abuse takes place both through the mediation of the children and enticement by agents.

Prevention and care

'Sri Lanka has a world-wide reputation for boy prostitution' according to a report in the *Economic Review* which went on to say that Sri Lanka is considered as a haven for those people who enjoy sex with children. Paedophile magazines which are published and circulated in Europe, advertise Sri Lanka in these terms. As long as Sri Lanka is so advertised, and the demand for child sex persists, the supply will continue to be met through local agents or pimps despite our efforts to curb it.

What happens to children who are sexually abused? What happens to their minds? What happens to their self-image? What happens to their future? Research shows that children exposed to sexual exploitation and pornography are almost impossible to rehabilitate. Our research has shown that only three per cent return to normal life in society through rehabilitation. Most of them have little schooling and those who were exposed to pornography are psychologically paralysed. They feel self-contempt and believe that even if they try to change their lives, it will only result in disaster. They have lost all sense of control over their lives and had accept a feeling of being trapped and victimized. They are psychosocially destroyed and are frequently drug addicts.

Sri Lanka ratified the Convention on the Rights of the Child on 12 July 1991 and adopted its own Children's Charter on the Rights of the Child. So the political commitment is there. But what action should be taken? The obvious thing to do is to increase awareness of the problem. The boys involved must be taught about the consequences of what they are doing, about the consequences of lack of schooling, of drugs, of crime which often follows, and about HIV and Aids, and that they are in fact risking their lives.

It is very encouraging to note the political will of the present government headed by Her Excellency Chandrika Bandaranaike Kumaratunga in its genuine efforts to curb the menace of commercial sexual exploitation of children. The establishment of the Presidential Task Force to combat child sexual abuse, the establishment of Child and Woman Desks in every police division in the charge of a woman police officer, the establishment of a hot line for informants of child sex abuse at police headquarters, the setting-up of a Task Force for the Elimination of Child Labour and amendments to the penal code are some of the progressive measures taken by the present government to arrest the problem of child sexual abuse in Sri Lanka. A Child Protection Authority is soon to be set up.

Even if laws are important, they alone will not suffice to curb commercial sexual exploitation of children. There has to be organized, multi-pronged, collective action through comprehensive strategies including community motivation, and commitment and dedication by child rights activists, grassroots organizations working in the field of children's rights, government departments such as Probation and Child Care Services, Immigration and Emigration, Health, Education and Social Services, the tourist and travel trade, hotel and tour operators, the police and the judiciary.

Any solution to the problem of commercial sexual exploitation of children and sexual abuse must address its root causes: poverty, dysfunctioning in the family unit, broken homes, migration of women abroad seeking employment, advertising abroad of Sri Lanka as a haven for child sexual exploitation. In addition, ways and means of eradicating sexual exploitation of children must also include education, creating awareness, gainful employment and recovery, and reintegration and rehabilitation of exploited and abused child victims.

Chapter 3

THE PHILIPPINES: FIGHTING CHILD ABUSE

Alex Corpus Hermoso and Father Shay Cullen

PREDA Social Development Foundation began as a centre for the rehabilitation of teenage youth offenders and drug dependants in Olongapo City, Subic Bay, the Philippines in 1974. It was set up by Father Shay Cullen in response to the social effects of the commercial sex industry that grew up around the huge United States Naval Station. Over the years the work expanded to include helping street children as well as sexually abused and exploited children, doing advocacy work and taking legal action against abusers, raising public awareness, and creating alternative economic livelihood opportunities for the young.

The 1970s was the period of martial law when the economic situation grew increasingly difficult for the rural poor. It was marked by land seizures and the growth of slums, while unemployment and poverty reached an unparalleled level. It should have been no surprise that thousands flocked to the perceived prosperity of Manila and the towns that surround the US military bases where our work began.

We learned that many political personalities were largely responsible for not only allowing the sexual exploitation of women and children, but also for promoting it for personal gain. The social conditions fostering this exploitation were a direct result of the economic and political decisions of local governments. Politicians were not only giving their consent by their silence but were also actively involved in setting up bars and clubs, issuing licences and permits, overlooking forged birth certificates of minors classified as adults, and by setting up and running venereal disease control programmes to make customers feel safer when sexually exploiting women and children.

In Asia, for example, commercial sexual exploitation of children typically takes the form of local men using the services of child prostitutes, or of so-called 'sex tourism'. Sometimes children are sold into the sex trade by families or friends, sometimes knowingly, sometimes in the mistaken belief that the children will become domestic servants or otherwise earn money for the family. Sometimes the children are kidnapped, trafficked across borders or from rural to urban areas, and moved from place to place so that they effectively 'disappear'. World Congress on the Commercial Sexual Exploitation of Children: Overview.

The industry was organized, controlled and efficient in its business of destroying human lives. From the roots of sex tourism and prostitution in military zones, a new destructive pattern of human degradation was imposed on the people. We regret to say that the situation is still very much the same today in the Philippines, just as it is in other parts of the world. We knew we were up against immense forces and powers that had deep vested interests in the commercialization of sexual services, especially those of children. Child pornography, we learned, was and is a massive industry in itself, that systematically promotes abuse of children. Today the full flowering of that sordid industry is gaining pervading presence in the new medium of communication and information dissemination, i.e., the Internet.

Rehabilitation work and legal action in favour of children

In 1989 we opened a residential recovery centre for sexually exploited and abused children. We did not content ourselves with providing a safe protective home but provided a therapeutic recovery programme. We thought it was essential to continue to expand advocacy work and provide a legal response focusing on the plight of street children and children in jail. Soon, we were able to get children released. Other children came to live at the PREDA residential centre for street children. Later, we were able to determine how many were sexually abused and in need of special therapy and assistance to recover. But legal action to combat the paedophilia scourge was just as necessary as the recovery work.

Our legal action began in a modest way with some local cases against United States servicemen and retirees. This had little success other than to expose the weakness of the legal system at the time and its inability to bring offenders to court. The lack of a child protection law was apparent. There was only one provision in the Philippine penal code that allowed prosecutions to succeed but they rarely did. Change came with the passage of the Child Protection Law in 1992 (Act 7610). The experience we gained allowed us to expand our lobbying for initiating new laws and legal practices in the Philippines and also abroad. The promotion of national and international networking with other concerned agencies and organizations became a priority. In 1990 we supported the ECPAT (End Child Prostitution in Asian Tourism) movement which aimed to bring about the passage of new extra-territorial and child pornography laws in Australia, Germany, Ireland, Japan, New Zealand and the United Kingdom. Such laws were passed not long ago, except in the case of Japan. We have continued our lobbying with the Japanese Diet.

Foreign paedophiles are protected by local bar and club operators, politicians and police. Direct legal action against these abusers is a risky but rewarding endeavour. It contributes greatly to public-awareness building. Our first successes entailed getting one of the first major convictions of a foreigner in the Philippines for the sexual exploitation of children, followed by the first conviction of a foreigner for offering minors for sexual exploitation to foreign sex tourists. Several more convictions followed. One of the more significant cases involved a Japanese sentenced to 42 years for molesting a group of street children. He was spreading child pornography, which he made himself, to induce children to have sex with him and with each other. His appeal was finally rejected in late 1998.

These cases were reported by the Philippine Government and NGOs to the UN-CRC Monitoring Committee. At present our investigations are focusing more and more on the Internet as a tool being used by paedophiles and child traffickers to entice foreigners to come to the Philippines. PREDA's legal action is hampered by an organized syndicate thought to be making and distributing child pornography on the Internet. This group is suspected of making locally produced pornographic material in bars and in the residences of foreign bar operators assisted by local collaborators. Gathering evidence is extremely difficult and has aroused the ire of the sex industry, notably against our efforts to monitor its activities in trafficking 'child brides' on the Internet under the guise of offering 'pen pals' on websites ostensibly seeking to meet foreign friends and who are described as teenagers of the 'marrying kind'.

> States Parties shall take all appropriate measures to ensure that children of working parents have the right to benefit from child-care services and facilities for which they are eligible. Article 18, United Nations Convention on the Rights of the Child.

In November 1998 PREDA assisted in uncovering sex tours being offered on the Internet. The website was closed down but the suspects operating in the United Kingdom and the Philippines have not been officially investigated. This is one of the major problems: the inability of the police to investigate Internet-based crimes. Combating child pornography, paedophilia and sexual exploitation of children on the Internet is now one of the greatest challenges, together with the sexual abuse of children at home and child exploitation in the sex industry.

PREDA is presently cooperating with other NGOs and law enforcement agencies to track advertising on the Internet of sextours offering minors, and in following these tours if and when they come to the Philippines. Other areas involve tracking down the operators behind child bride schemes, another method of enticing foreign paedophiles seeking out minors for sexual exploitation. PREDA has a constructive dialogue with the Philippine Internet service providers to monitor their servers and voluntarily undertake to provide proxy servers to schools and homes to prevent children from accessing pornographic websites from home- or school-based computers.

Chapter 4

KENYA: REVEALING CHILD ABUSE

Philista Onyango

Awareness of child abuse in Kenya, and the efforts to combat it, were focused initially on child labour and go back to the colonial era. Missionaries found in the 1930s that child labour on European farms or in domestic service generated negative social effects in the form of disorderliness, alcohol abuse and the breakdown of traditional respect for elders. As a result, in Kenya, changes in colonial legislation regarding child labour were introduced as early as 1936.

More comprehensive studies of the extent and impact of child labour were, however, only carried out in the mid-1980s. These revealed not only the very wide extent of the problem but also highlighted problems of physical and sexual abuse. These studies pointed to the disintegration of the traditional African extended family system – long portrayed as caring and protective of children – to the point that it was becoming a threat to children. The majority of children working in domestic service were being enticed with promises of free education. In reality, few children received the promised education and were in fact reduced to what could only be called conditions of slavery.

> In Africa, evidence suggests that the employment of children as domestic servants often includes sexual exploitation. There are also indications that children are employed in hotels, restaurants and brothels, where they are sexually exploited. Additionally, there is evidence of commercial sexual exploitation of children – particularly girls – in refugee camps, where the large number of single men assembled in one place drives demand for sex, and of exploitation of camp children by men in surrounding communities. This same phenomenon underlies the evidence of children – this time often young boys – recruited into the armed forces not only to fight but to service the soldiers. In many parts of Africa, governments continue to deny that the problem exists. World Congress on the Commercial Sexual Exploitation of Children: Overview.

Parents increasingly saw their children as the only way to escape poverty, and the first thing to be sacrificed was primary school education. Even though during the 1980s primary school education was officially free, parents were reporting that they could not afford obligatory school uniforms or diverse school levies. In many cases, education for young girls was being sacrificed in favour of education for boys. Relatives in urban areas on the other hand were using children as cheap labour where they could not afford adult labour or proper, affordable day care. In the space of a few years in the early 1980s, street girls – prostitutes and beggars – began to become increasingly visible in Nairobi. Studies involving these girls revealed that a large number had been in domestic service but had run away to escape physical and sexual abuse by their employers. Life on the streets was exposing these children to harmful influences totally foreign to traditional African codes of conduct.

Alarming population growth rates and declining economic performance caused increasing numbers of young people to leave their rural homes in search of jobs and education opportunities in urban centres. The majority of these had dropped out of school and were unskilled. Internationally funded structural adjustment programmes also impacted heavily on poor families when subsidies for many services were cut, including schooling. A study carried out in Kenya in 1991 revealed that 300,000 school-age children were not in school. Despite the country having attained almost universal primary education in the mid-1980s, by 1995 school enrolment of 6 to 13 year olds had slipped to 76 per cent. With so many children out of school, situations of exploitation and social abuse were increasing and taking new forms. More and more children were on the streets engaged in prostitution or carrying out exploitative work on plantations and in domestic service.

The response: setting up an African network

Similar developments were taking place throughout Africa, aggravated in many countries by war and civil conflicts which have generated very large numbers of displaced children. In 1985 the first conference on child abuse in Africa was held, involving sixteen countries. The meeting clearly demonstrated that child abuse was rampant and there was need for a network to begin to focus on and deal with the problem. A second meeting in 1986 of 22 countries considered child abuse in its broadest terms, including the impact of armed conflicts, famine and widely prevalent cultural traditions such as female circumcision. Out of this meeting was born the African Network for the Prevention and Protection against Child Abuse and Neglect (ANPPCAN) aimed at encouraging research as a means of influencing policy-making and implementation in the participating countries.

Over the years, ANPPCAN has coordinated major studies on abuse of exploitation of children. National chapters have carried out research on street children, violence and children, disability and child abuse, conflicts and children, corporal punishment of children, children and criminal justice, and child abuse in urban and rural settings. A recent study has examined the effects of structural adjustment and social policy reforms, and the risks of violence among urban adolescents.

ANPPCAN has mobilized support from international organizations such as the OAU and UNICEF and has organized regional and continent-wide meetings on various topics including: child abuse and children in especially difficult circumstances (1985), child labour (1986), the Draft Convention on the Rights of the Child and the African Charter on the Rights and Welfare of the Child (1988), sub-regional workshops on children and conflicts (1994–96), and a Continental Conference on the Impact of Armed Conflicts on Children (1997).

> States Parties shall take all appropriate measures to promote physical and psychological recovery and social reintegration of a child victim of: any form of neglect, exploitation, or abuse; torture or any other form of cruel, inhuman or degrading treatment or punishment; or armed conflicts. Such recovery and reintegration shall take place in an environment which fosters the health, self respect and dignity of the child. Article 39, United Nations Convention on the Rights of the Child.

In Kenya, the ANPPCAN Regional Office has sought to play a coordinating role, for example by participating in the creation of a Coalition on Child Rights and Child Protection, and by bringing together four key government ministries and four broadly based NGOs. Reporting Centres on Child Abuse have been created in Nairobi, as well as a Children's Legal Action Network and a Child in Need Network.

ANPPCAN has also been active in supporting and empowering communities to fight for the rights of children. For example, in Kenya, the Regional Office in Nairobi has started a programme on community organization and child protection in slum communities. Community and family-based day-care centres have also been created to cater for children aged from 3 to 7 years.

Chapter 5

BRAZIL: FAMILY, SOCIAL AND ECONOMIC PERSPECTIVES, ORIGINS, CAUSES, PREVENTION AND CARE

Hélia Barbosa

Brazil's vast territory (8 million square kilometres) and population (164 million inhabitants of which 40 per cent are under 18), its economic, cultural and geographical diversity, even the politics of the country and its regions, make it difficult to analyse the problem of sexual abuse and exploitation. In socioeconomic terms, Brazil is a land of stark contrasts. A rich country with a poor population, it ranks 8th in the world economy but 74th in terms of quality of life. Although it is the 5th greatest world food producer, its population is generally undernourished and many die of hunger. Some 20 million inhabitants are indigent and 40 million children and adolescents are inadequately cared for, if not abandoned. About 4 million children under the age of 14 work. The 44 per cent mortality rate for children under the age of five 5 places Brazil in 84th position worldwide. Millions of children are not in school. Many are siblings of individuals who are already socially excluded, and a first generation of children born on the streets inhabits Brazil's major cities, despite the numerous programmes to assist adolescent mothers in precarious situations.

> In Guatemala, you get a longer jail sentence for stealing a car than for stealing a baby. If you want sexy young girls for prostitution in Canada, you can get them from Costa Rica. If you are an enterprising foreigner in Honduras, you can set up a bar and offer little Honduran girls for sex to the other visiting foreign tourists. Or in Costa Rica, if you are a tourist, you can buy sex from little girls, but often in the morning, as they have to go to primary school in the afternoon . . . . Bruce

Harris, Casa Alianza, Presentation to the 24th Session of the United Nations Working Group on Contemporary Forms of Slavery, Geneva, 24 June 1999.

There are no reliable statistics on the number of children and adolescents who are victims of abuse and sexual exploitation. However, it is all too apparent that the low sociocultural and economic indicators point – for reasons of sheer survival – to sexual exploitation of children and adolescents, particularly in the suburbs and centres of the big cities, as well as in rural areas and Indian communities that living alongside white ones. The major economic, political and social crises experienced by Brazilian society have lead to impoverishment, increasing social exclusion and privation of fundamental rights. The concentration of riches in the hands of relatively few people, to the detriment of the welfare of the majority of Brazilians continues to sustain the nation's unjust social structure.

In this context, traffic and commerce in sex subsists and grows by exploiting the misery of famished families. The majority of girls and adolescents who engage in prostitution do so simply to survive. They are part of the most vulnerable segment of the social pyramid. Their total lack of either personal or social prospects allows them to be easily induced or seduced by unscrupulous adults, exploited by middlemen and violated by 'clients'. Millions of Brazilian girls and adolescents exchange sexual favours for food and shelter, notwithstanding the fact that in these cases, the client of the girl or the person facilitating the commerce of her body can be sent to prison. This commerce flourishes in the great urban centres, in small communities and, increasingly, along the highways. Throughout Brazil's immense territory, in extremely poor regions girls are sold, sometimes by their own families, or simply kidnapped, to furnish sex where there are large concentrations of men such as mines or building sites. In Brazil, the highest rates of sexual exploitation are the riverside towns in Amazonas; the areas of miscegenation among whites and Indians; in the gold mining regions in the north-east, both in the arid regions of the back country and the coast; in areas where the tourist industry prospers or where child labour is used in the fields and in extraction industries; near international frontiers, especially with Paraguay and Bolivia; and in popular tourist cities such as Manaus, Fortaleza, Salvador, Ilhéus, Porto Seguro, Rio de Janeiro, Foz de Iguaçu and Florianopolis.

Yet misery is not the only thing that drives girls and boys to marginality. Allured by promises of a job and better opportunities in bigger cities, many adolescents leave their small districts and end up as virtual slaves in brothels, where they suffer all kinds of violence. Others, in the hope of earning good wages, or 'social climbing', or becoming a success and finding 'Prince Charming' let themselves be taken to other countries, mainly Switzerland, Germany and Spain, where they become a 'members' of international sexual exploitation networks, as has been widely divulged by the press.

Specific prevention programmes for sexual abuse and exploitation are still not sufficiently developed in Brazil. This was demonstrated at the recent Meeting of ECPAT when only 18 social and public entities were shown to be active in this area. While some of these programmes have had excellent results, they still do not meet to the needs of the greatest number of victims.

Examples of prevention strategies being applied in Brazil which reflect the current international consensus on combating sexual abuse of children include: alerting and sensitizing people through training in human rights and disseminating this awareness widely; fighting all forms of violence through efforts to ensure enforcement of the law and punishment of the guilty; making infant juvenile sexual abuse and exploitation a crime and using the law to prosecute the guilty and protect the innocent; establishing networks and alliances as well as programmes with a strong multidisciplinary base; organizing publicity, information and communication campaigns; building capacity in community leadership to sensitize and educate inhabitants at the local level; reinforcing self-protection and self-management of their rights; and creating and multiplying centres of informal education.

> State Parties recognize the right of the child to be protected from economic exploitation and from performing any work that is likely to be hazardous or to interfere with the child's education, or to be harmful to the child's health or physical, mental, spiritual, moral or social development. Article 32, United Nations Convention on the Rights of the Child.

The experience of articulation and mobilization to combat burgeoning infant and juvenile sexual exploitation in Bahia, Brazil, was the first example of a joint social action to show concrete results. The methodology and different stages of this process have been diffused to small districts and states, as well as at national and international levels. The CEDECA/Bahia initiative and its partners, mobilizing the civil society of Bahia at all levels, broke the silence around infant juvenile sexual exploitation.

Now recognized as one of Brazil's most grave national problems, this great social sore was exposed to the eyes of the nation by means of the National Campaign Against Infant Juvenile Sexual Exploitation launched in July 1995 in Bahia and then in October across all of the national territories by the President of the Republic. Its continuity was ensured by the National Programme of Human Rights of the Ministry of Justice of the Federal Government. This mobilization resulted in various other campaigns (numbering some 10 in different regions) as well as the National Campaign to End Exploitation, Violence and Sexual Tourism against Adolescents and Children. Brazil's vast area and social, economic and regional cultural diversity necessitated this process. Today there is a national debate on the subject, favoured by the active interest of the media, including television programmes at peak times.

Another interesting aspect was the adhesion to the cause of high-school and university students and teachers, transport workers, truck drivers and show-business unions. Some state legislatures set up parliamentary commissions of enquiry to assess the situation of sexual violence. Other actions are being developed by NGOs and associations. These are considered significant victories in the battle against sexual violence, although they may seem to be small efforts in the eyes of the public, in view of the seriousness of the problem.

Other recent initiatives include: the strengthening of the Denunciation System via the SOS Programmes; creation of special police units to investigate sexual crimes; establishment of temporary homes for mothers and children, who are victims of sexual abuse; provision of psychosocial care services for victims; creation of data banks; publications (books, brochures, newspapers, folders); training courses in human and children's rights, citizenship and sexuality for students, educators, justice and health professionals, tutors, counsellors, police, families and communities; and the creation of commissions and debate forums and joint ventures with universities.

Also worthy of note are the creation and implementation of specialized criminal courts for children and youth to prosecute and judge crimes against children and adolescents, which now exist in the states of Pernambuco and Bahia and could lead to a breakthrough against the impunity of these criminals. The court of Bahia has launched a pioneer activity in Brazil, a joint venture with CEDECA-Bahia to offer psychotherapy to the victims of sexual crimes.

Chapter 6

ALBANIA: NEW HOPE FOR ABUSED CHILDREN

Aurela Pano

The Children's Human Rights Centre of Albania (CRCA) is a group of lawyers, journalists, writers and physicians who, in March 1997, joined together in a commitment to children's rights in Albania, in line with the articles of the United Nations Convention of the Rights of the Child which was recognized by the Albanian Government and ratified by Parliament in February 1992.

The group's *raison d'être* is the protection of the rights of children in Albania. It is concerned with: legal protection of children's rights, on the basis of national and international law; raising awareness of the situation of children's rights in Albania; monitoring the social, health and education rights of Albanian children; and implementing statutes and legislation in support of the mother and child. Some of the Centre's major activities concern the implementation of Albanian legislation on children and the United Nations Convention on the Rights of the Child. It works in partnership with state bodies to fulfil its mission and objectives. It also works with non-governmental organizations whose main aim is the protection of children's rights. In this regard, a number of projects have been completed while others are still being implemented. Projects implemented to date include: publication of a leaflet on children's rights; a quarterly bulletin on the rights of children and youth; a national study on the reasons why children leave school; a national study on underage employment; a draft national law on the protection of children in Albania; organization of a children's concert with participants from Northern Ireland; delivery of aid for children donated by the people of Northern Ireland; and a radio programme on abused children.

In Europe, children are trafficked across the borders of mainland Europe from poorer countries in the East to wealthier countries where the market for children is fuelled by organised paedophile rings and high-tech information services. World Congress on the Commercial Sexual Exploitation of Children: Overview.

Owing to the absence of any previous study on how issues affecting children are covered in the press and, more generally, perceived by the public, the CRCA felt it was vital to prepare and complete such a study at national level and to establish data that could benefit children's protection groups and governmental bodies both in the country and in other countries. But, in monitoring the press, we found it difficult to locate references to the wide range of activities undertaken on behalf of children. Instead, we were confronted with a huge number of stories reporting crimes against children, including murder, rape, incest, assault, paedophilia and smuggling of children to neighbouring countries for prostitution.

When a child is abused there are no suitable facilities where that child can go for advice or help. Considering that these crimes are very traumatic for the victims, the CRCA feels that some form of counselling should be available to those who need it. This is why the CRCA would like to establish a centre in Albania where children could receive advice for mental, physical, emotional and especially sexual abuse problems. We hope to achieve this in the not the too distant future and are seeking donations to assist in funding the project.

The Internet

In Tirana and Albania on the whole the Internet has had very little impact, mainly because of the lack of access to equipment and the small number of available servers. At the time of writing, there have been no reported cases of Internet-related sexual abuse of children in Albania, if only because the open nature of the Internet makes it very difficult to uncover the extent of such cases. Nevertheless, the CRCA recognizes the potential future problem for abuse on the Internet and feels that some measures should be put into place *now* to help protect minors from such abuse.

Chapter 7

GROUND-LEVEL REALITIES AND INTERNATIONAL ACTION: A VITAL ROLE OF NGOS

Hélène Sackstein

If the 1996 Stockholm World Congress against the Commercial Sexual Exploitation of Children was successful, it was partly because of the scope and the effectiveness of the role played by NGOs. Not only did they interact and network strongly among themselves, but a particularly potent chemistry developed among the organizers of the event, i.e., the Government of Sweden, UNICEF, the international ECPAT (End Child Prostitution in Asian Tourism) campaign, and the NGO Group for the Convention on the Rights of the Child, consisting of some 44 NGOs, both large and small, sharing a commitment to the rights of children. The new technologies, notably the Internet, under discussion today in order to find ways of controlling their negative uses, continue to have a very positive impact in the promotion of networking and the strengthening of partnerships which will give results on the ground and an effective voice at international level.

> What is beyond doubt, however, is that worldwide children are being sold into sex. It has been estimated that every year one million children are in the sex trade, exploited by people or by circumstance. World Congress on the Commercial Sexual Exploitation of Children : Overview.

The magnitude and complexity of the problem of child sex abuse, as well as the will to sustain the momentum generated in Stockholm, spurred the creation of the Support Group on the Sexual Exploitation of Children. The NGO Group for the Convention on the Rights of the Child was designated as the Focal Point to facilitate information sharing, and encourage collabora-tive initiatives and input into international monitoring mechanisms. Essen-tially, the NGO Group, through the Focal Point Programme, serves as a sort of two-way conveyor belt between a growing number of Support Group members – comprising interested governments, United Nations Agencies, NGOs, research institutions and individual experts – and international mon-itoring mechanisms such as the Committee on the Rights of the Child and the United Nations Special Rapporteur. In the process it facilitates the iden-tification of sources of technical assistance and best practices, the evaluation of programmes, capacity building and co-funding initiatives. The Focal Point Programme is the instrument through which linkages and networking among all these players are maintained and developed. It is a loose association of fully autonomous members. The Focal Point Programme has no advocacy activities, leaving this task to individual members.

While promoting greater cooperation, it is hoped that the Focal Point experience will also help to reduce duplication and limit costs. It might also serve as a precedent and pave the way for similar collaborative initiatives on other child rights and/or human rights issues, hence providing more inte-grated support to all relevant international monitoring mechanisms.

A complex and cross-cutting issue

Having dealt with the process for the follow-up to the World Congress, it might be worthwhile to briefly recall some of the points raised in Stockholm in 1996, as the issue of sexual exploitation is still confused in the mind of the pub-lic and is much more complex than is generally assumed. It goes well beyond the prostitution and sex tourism which have been given a high degree of visi-bility in the media. Furthermore, no aspect of sexual abuse or exploitation of children can be dealt with in a vacuum. This is particularly true in the case of the expanding plague of child abuse through pornography on the Internet.

As for paedophilia, although it is certainly a contributing factor to sexual abuse of children, it certainly cannot be considered as the main cause. Both are more likely to be the insidious consequences of a widespread malignant cancer, in a world where human progress has not been able to keep up with the advances of technology and the pressures of market forces. The main fight is against child abuse in all its forms.

It is not possible to obtain precise figures on the extent of child prostitu-tion. However, in 1996, the United Nations Special Rapporteur on the Sale of Children, Child Prostitution and Child Pornography estimated that one million children in Asia alone are victims of the sex trade. With the new eco-nomic crisis in several Asian countries, this figure must be a vast underesti-mation. It is even more difficult to obtain reliable data on child victims of other forms of sexual abuse and violence, particularly within the family. To underscore the latter point, in 1998, the British Broadcasting Corporation (BBC) news noted that a hotline for children in distress in the United Kingdom had recorded over one million calls in the preceding year, an increase of 12 per cent over the previous year. These calls came from children fearing physical and sexual violence by family members or people close to them, for themselves, their siblings or friends.

In step with an expanding global economy, trafficking in children and adolescents under the age of 18 for sexual exploitation purposes is a global and sophisticated market, with links to arms and drugs networks, as well as to legitimate businesses through money laundering. A 1995 United Nations report estimated that globally, child prostitution nets US$5 billion annually. Although girls represent the vast majority of the victims, the number of boys is increasing and, in some countries (e.g., Sri Lanka), surpasses the number of girls. It would appear that the 'sex industry' is more lucrative than the drug or arms markets and is much safer for its 'managers' because the penalties for those who are caught remain far lower than for other forms of illicit trade. Sad to say, human beings, and children in particular, are an easy merchandise to commercialize.

This type of market is, like all markets, based on supply and demand. So far, all attention has focused on the supply side (the child victims). However, much more thought should be given to the demand side (the ordinary consumers, the pimps and procurers, i.e., the managers, not simply the paedophiles). This has implications for issues such as the content of education for boys as well as girls, and a whole range of other areas of concern to child rights advocates. The 1996 Stockholm World Congress clearly established that commercial sexual exploitation and sexual abuse of children have a multitude of common causes: poverty, consumerism, breakdown of communal values through armed conflicts, economic upheavals brought about by the globalization process and structural adjustment policies, and so forth. Both involve abuse of power or of authority on the part of an adult or an older child and, beyond this, by the haves over the have-nots.

The widespread sexual abuse and exploitation of children and their trivialization are symptoms of a serious and deep dysfunction within a community or society, affecting all aspects of child rights, and they challenge us to consider innovative and integrated, multidisciplinary measures of prevention, protection and treatment to combat them. National and grassroots NGOs in various regions of the world have frequently stressed that sexual abuse, violence and exploitation of children are not problems which can be taken in isolation, but rather that they cut across many other social and legal issues such as drug abuse, child labour, street children, juvenile justice, gender, minority and racial discrimination, and health factors such as the HIV/Aids pandemic and other STDs. Studies have demonstrated that sexually abused and exploited children tend to grow into adults who continue to be exploited or become offenders themselves. The implication of this exponential multiplication of potential victims and offenders is evident. In an era when many governments' actions are determined by financial considerations, efforts should be made to calculate the costs of inaction to society. The resulting figures might lead to more sustained and concerted prevention efforts on the part of governments.

Conclusion

The World Congress succeeded in placing concern about the sexual exploitation of children on the world's social agenda and making it everybody's business. One less obvious, but no less important, achievement was to contribute to the realization by all participants that, in our global village, it is no longer possible to hoard information, ideas, programmes and initiatives. At the end of the day, the international community realized that to tackle issues as widespread as the sexual exploitation of children, indeed, all human rights violations, it needed to seriously share, cooperate and collaborate at all levels; internationally, nationally and locally, and that states, civil society, academia and so on, have to go beyond soothing words and good intentions.

The Focal Point Programme is attempting to ensure that it provides some of the ingredients needed to strengthen the links among actors in this arduous combat. Partnerships need to be as broad-based as possible and the private sector has not yet been sufficiently mobilized. Indeed, nor have the institutions of the global market economy so far shown sufficient interest in what is timidly called the 'social clause'.

> States Parties shall take all appropriate national, bilateral and multilateral measures to prevent the abduction of, the sale of or traffic in *children for* any purpose or in any form. Article 35, United Nations Convention on the Rights of the Child.

As for the Internet, it is clear that more efforts must be made to engage the industry, and in particular access providers, in this fight. National legislation, no matter how comprehensive, is not equipped to deal with cyberspace, and new means of international cooperation need to be invented. NGOs are already dealing with this issue at all levels and it is an uphill battle. More needs to be done to convince all the actors in this struggle that all human rights are equal and indivisible and that freedom of expression is not a right superior to the right of a child to dignity, physical integrity and protection – as stipulated in the United Nations Convention on the Rights of the Child. A balance needs to be struck, and compromises worked out, to ensure that all these rights are equally protected. The ultimate test is one of political will. Here, NGOs have a vital role to play in holding their governments accountable.

CHILD PORNOGRAPHY AND PAEDOPHILIA: ATTEMPTING A DEFINITION

Child pornography

The question of what constitutes child pornography is complex. The standards applied are often subjective and contingent upon moral, cultural, sexual, social and religious beliefs that differ from one culture to another, from one country to another and even among different societies in the same country. Furthermore, these mores do not readily translate into law in the strictly juridical sense. Legal definitions of both children and child pornography differ globally and may differ among legal jurisdictions within the same country. However, the United Nations Convention on the Rights of the Child, which has now been adopted by 191 Member States, provides a universal definition of the child as any person under the age of eighteen years.

The 1996 Stockholm World Congress against the Commercial Sexual Exploitation of Children defined child pornography as 'any visual or audio material which uses children in a sexual context. It consists of the visual depiction of a child engaged in explicit sexual conduct, real or simulated, or the lewd exhibition of the genitals intended for the sexual gratification of the user, and involves the production, distribution and/or use of such material'.

> States Parties shall use their best efforts to ensure recognition of the principle that both parents have common responsibilities for the upbringing and development of the child. Parents or, as the case may be, legal guardians, have the primary responsibility for the upbringing and development of the child. The best interests of the child will be their basic concern. Article 18, United Nations Convention on the Rights of the Child.

The United Nations Special Rapporteur on the sale of children, child prostitution and child pornography defines visual child pornography (as distinguished from audio child pornography) as the 'visual depiction of a child, real or simulated, engaged in explicit sexual activity, or the lewd exhibition of genitals, and involves the production, distribution and/or use of such material.' In this definition, 'real or simulated' is placed right after 'child' to make it clear that it also pertains to pseudo-imaging or 'morphing' of the child. The phrase 'for the sexual gratification of the user' is not used, given the difficulty of its interpretation. In other words, child pornography is described in terms of the act alone, regardless of its 'benefits' to the user.

The Council of Europe defines child pornography in very broad terms as 'any audiovisual material which uses children in a sexual context'. The International Criminal Police Organization (Interpol) defines child pornography as the 'visual depiction of the sexual exploitation of a child, focusing on the child's sexual behaviour or genitals'. For the purposes of determining the criminal nature of the offence in clear terms, this definition is perhaps necessary, even 'helpful'.

Paedophilia

Most dictionaries define *paedophilia* as a sexual attraction or preference for prepubescent children, usually under the age of thirteen. As this is usually understood as a psychiatric description, law enforcement agents often employ a broader definition of paedophilia to include adults who are sexually attracted to persons legally considered as children.

In some jurisdictions, e.g., France, the word 'paedophilia' appears nowhere in the civil or criminal codes. Certain French medical literature remains ambiguous about the nature of paedophilia, not classifying it explicitly as an illness, whether physical or psychological. It is perceived more as a sexual 'orientation' towards young children, harmless if it remains in the realm of fantasy, but perverse if it leads to a sexual act involving a child.

The Child Sex Abuser: ECPAT's operational definition

Persons who exploit children sexually, in the view of ECPAT, fall into two categories: the true paedophile or 'preferential child sex abuser' and the 'situational child sex abuser'. One category suffers from a personality disorder; the abusers in the other category are experimenting with new forms of sexual contact.

In the paper prepared by Julia O'Connell Davidson for the World Congress against the Commercial Sexual Exploitation of Children, she describes both of these categories. The first two pages of her paper are summarized and paraphrased below.

The term 'paedophile' is a clinical one, used to refer to an adult who has a personality disorder which involves a specific and focused sexual interest in prepubescent children. The majority of paedophiles are male, but female abusers are not unknown, and though some paedophiles have a focused interest in either female or male victims, others have no consistent gender preference. Paedophiles do not all act on their sexual interest in the same way. Some restrict their sexual life to fantasy. Those who do act upon their impulses may abuse children in a variety of ways, some limiting themselves to non-contact abuse, others perpetrating contact abuse. The 'preferential child sex abusers' are abusers who are usually, but not always, men, and their victims may be either male or female children. Psychiatry views their taste for immature and powerless sexual partners as the manifestation of a personality disorder (hebephilia).

Paedophiles and preferential child sex abusers do not constitute a homogeneous group in terms of how they operate. Three major behaviour patterns have been identified. The 'seduction pattern' is followed by offenders who are motivated by a form of narcissism; these offenders will groom their victims perhaps over long periods of time, and will use threats and blackmail to discourage disclosure. The 'introverted' offenders have a preference for children, but lack the interpersonal skills of the seducer; these offenders will tend to abuse very young children. The 'sadistic' offenders derive sexual pleasure from the infliction of pain on their victims; they are more likely to abduct and murder their victims than any other type of offender.

The second category, the 'situational child sex abusers' are men and women who sexually exploit children, not because they have a sexual interest in children *per se*, but because they are morally and/or sexually indiscriminate and want to experiment. Or they may have entered into situations in which children who match their ideals of physical attraction are sexually accessible to them and there are certain disinhibiting factors present which allow them to delude themselves about the child's age, or the nature of the child's consent. These abusers do not consciously seek out children as sexual partners, but use them when such children are available.

Generally child pornography will be possessed, made and distributed by the paedophile or preferential sex abuser. However, it would appear from a number of arrests in recent months that the ease with which child pornography can be accessed on the Internet, and its anonymity, has meant that 'situational' child sex abusers are also using child pornography via this medium.

Chapter 8

PAEDOPHILIA: A PSYCHIATRIC AND PSYCHOANALYTICAL POINT OF VIEW

Patrice Dunaigre

From the standpoint of psychiatry and psychoanalysis, it has been observed that, although paedophilia has always existed, in fact it has never been 'institutionalized', i.e., considered admissible for the purpose of regulating relations between the social and the sexual spheres. As a consequence, it is condemned to remain simultaneously marginal, but present wherever the social order is built on the incest taboo. This is borne out by the fact that it is not exclusive to any given culture, society, level of development or class.

One modern psychoanalytical point of view sees paedophilia as a crisis that strikes at the heart of the content of systems of kinship. The particular resonance triggered by paedophilia could, perhaps, stem from the present upheaval that kinship structures are themselves experiencing. The child thus 'naturally' becomes the focal point on which to base any analysis of the questions at issue in the social debate encompassing not only the crisis in parental authority; transmission of knowledge; reconstituted families; 'new couples'; misgivings surrounding medically assisted procreation techniques; recognition of homosexuality as an accepted component of society; and abortion rights, but also the possibility of children's access to sex education and the spread of Aids. All of these are questions, which, by making the child their central focus, exacerbate those issues that specifically affect children.

The paedophile and the child as scapegoats of the projections triggered by this crisis

The paedophile is an emblematic figure, made into a caricature and imbued with all the fears, anxieties and apprehensions rocking our society today. It should be noted in passing that these fears are by nature very close to those of which the child is the catalyst. The result is a blurring of exactly about whom and what one is talking. One need look no further than the tone used in the media coverage of sexual abuse of children where accusations are levelled not only against the adult aggressor (in this case the paedophile) but also against 'caretakers', who are blamed for incapacity or powerlessness, and against the 'authorities', charged with incompetence, laxness or even duplicity. The victim – the child – is reduced simply to being the object of the act perpetrated.

This non-attention to the child-victim is in keeping with a stereotype, that of the child considered to be an inconsequential, irresponsible creature, a mere object of power or desire, a one-dimensional surface onto which all sorts of fantasies can be projected. In the end, this reduces the child to silence.

Therefore, since the child cannot speak, the media will assume the role of mouthpiece in talking about the paedophile. After having been nowhere, the paedophile will now be suspected of being everywhere, and, more particularly, wherever societal fears and concerns are most acutely focused: in places where knowledge is imparted to the child (schools and various institutions); in individuals holding positions of authority or respectability; in socially marginal places, in trains, train stations, at the baker's shop, and so on and so forth.

Emerging from this are mugshots of the paedophile that lock him into an imaginary typology and close off all possibilities for further examination of the transgression of which he is the author. Even if, by vilifying the paedophile, society as a body can exorcise its fears, this attitude contributes nothing either to the understanding of the phenomenon or to its prevention. This is all the more worrying as vilifying the aggressor is tantamount to 'infantilizing' the victim. Moreover, any strategy based on an imaginary precept (albeit a politically expedient one) runs the risk of treating the victim as an indistinct entity and of perpetuating the ignorance of the paedophile and thus the understanding of the very nature of the paedophilic act.

Describing paedophilic behaviours is not sufficient for their understanding but only makes it possible to define their specificity. The aim is also to exclude certain behaviours which, in the present climate, are wrongly classified as paedophilic. Lastly, careful analysis of paedophilia scenarios provides useful information for prevention purposes.

A clinical definition

According to the World Health Organization (WHO), paedophile acts are sexual behaviours that an adult major (16 years or over), essentially of the male sex, acts out towards prepubescent children (13 years or under). There must normally be a five-year age difference between the two, except in the case of paedophilic practices at the end of adolescence where what counts is more the difference in sexual maturity.

A few general characteristics complete the definition: some paedophiles prefer boys and others girls, while still others are aroused by both sexes. Those who are attracted to girls tend to select children aged between eight and ten years old, whereas those who prefer boys like them to be slightly older. A distinction is made between the exclusive type of paedophile who is sexually attracted to children only, and the non-exclusive type of paedophile who can also be sexually active with adults.

Paedophile behaviour varies, ranging from exhibitionism without physical contact to acts of penetration aimed (or not) at sexual zones. To achieve their ends, paedophiles sometimes use different means as well as different degrees of coercion. Paedophilia primarily involves male perpetrators.

General classification

Situational paedophilia: Some adults sexually assault children without necessarily feeling any real sexual attraction towards them. These are often isolated, impulsive acts committed by individuals with pathological personalities.

Preferential paedophilia: This is the conventional form of paedophilia that involves sexual deviance regarding prepubescent children, acted out in various forms. It can be described using criteria such as sexual preference, exclusive or non-exclusive type, type of sexual offence, strategies used, ways of perpetration, character traits, weak or strong social competences, and so on. It is important to note that paedophilia is found in all sociocultural milieus and social classes, from the poorest to the richest, and that a paedophile is not a hirsute, dirty character lurking in the dark, waiting to pounce. On the contrary, he can be someone who is a friend to all, often well integrated in society and, sometimes, entirely above suspicion. This last criterion, however, is not always specific to the paedophile. It is, at most, an indication that he never talks about or openly displays his paedophilic tendencies.

Sexual practices between an adult and an adolescent and sexual aggression against young majors do not fall within the confines of paedophilia. In this regard, the age criterion is a strict prerequisite. Victims must be under thirteen years old. This has been very well documented in the North American literature through the 'Relapse Prevention Model'. It is interesting because it gives an account of the different factors that culminate in the actual act being carried out from its beginnings to the end. One can therefore distinguish between:

> *Pre-attack emotional factors:* The appearance of a depressive state, an anxious feeling of boredom, a sense of failure and powerlessness are often reported by paedophiles as precursors of a rise in their deviant sexual arousal. They lead to an orchestration of a paedophile scenario.

> *Rational factors:* In preferential paedophilia, the actual act is very rarely carried out on impulse. It can usually be broken down into precise sequences: a relational strategy, an approach strategy, risk assessment, carrying out of the act.

This latter involves a process developed over varying lengths of time. It requires the establishment of relations either with the family or with the entourage of the child selected. Victims are selected on the basis of personal criteria such as gender, age and general physical characteristics. Initial contact is made using various stratagems, ranging from conversation, gifts, display of interest in the child's likes or hobbies, to the use of threats and force. Pornographic material may be used. The paedophile constantly assesses the risk involved. He therefore takes into account such factors as the presence or absence of potential witnesses, possible denunciation by the child, the supposed reaction of parents or relatives and close associates, revenge, reporting to the police, and so on. Knowledge of this process, analysed on the basis of the theory of rational choice, makes it possible to provide prevention officers with relatively reliable information on the strategies used by paedophiles.

Treatment of the paedophile

The paedophile scenario has evolved into a paradox that seeks to radicalize the breakdown of the link established between sexuality and the various legalities that serve to maintain a dimension in sexual relations that one might call symbolic. Though this dimension takes many forms that may vary considerably from one society or culture to another, its need is always affirmed. By imposing a lawless sexuality, the paedophile totally undermines the symbolic dimension of sexuality.

As a consequence, the penal dimension is justified because the act of paedophilia is a criminal act in the sense that it represents a threat to a humanizing principle that is fundamental for society. In the case of paedophilia, this preventive measure (in the sense of securing oneself from danger) is supplemented, in certain societies, by mandatory sentencing to undergo treatment, if only with a view to prevention of relapses about which there are, let it be said in passing, no reliable statistics.

Various systems of 'persuasion' to convince people of the need for treatment have thus been put in place. Without going into the detail of the dialectics developed, all the systems are aimed at either encouraging or compelling the paedophile to take cognizance of his problems.

There are two main types of treatment:

Psychological therapies: These therapies have in common their emphasis on the importance of controlling the effects. Those based on cognitive-behaviourist theories focus on facilitating development of, the sometimes deficient, social competences and skills. Systemic-based therapies seek to create group dynamics. There are also some therapies which centre on analysis of the patient's social network or history. It is very difficult to determine the effectiveness of these treatments mainly because they are conducted essentially in a prison setting or as a result of a sentence. It is possible that they are of genuine benefit to some paedophiles.

Drug-based therapies: Anti-androgen hormonal treatments are reputed to be effective on the impulsive component of unwanted, deviant sexual fantasies (and therefore reduce or eliminate the temptation to carry out acts of sexual aggression). Their effectiveness ceases as soon as the patient stops taking them.

In attempting to respond to the question of whether treatment is effective, one would be well-advised to ask another question, i.e., whether the conditions under which treatment currently takes place are appropriate to the specific issues posed by paedophilia – a question that for the moment is very difficult to answer given the dearth of sufficiently elaborate information. What is certain is that the notion of treatment is essentially based on the notion of relapse prevention, a much too general concept that does not fully grasp the diversity of paedophile conduct and which reduces the subject to his act. It should be noted here that a penal code is not a public health policy.

Rehabilitation of offenders

The rehabilitation of offenders poses a major challenge especially for those for whom predilection for sex with children is compulsive in nature. Treatment required for this type of abnormal behaviour is quite expensive and of doubtful effectiveness. The well-based assumption that any punitive measure imposed upon the offender will not preclude a repetition of the same offence raises fears close to panic in some countries.

Among the 'curative' remedies being tried in some countries are medical castration and lobotomy. Others require the publication of the names and pictures of the offender and the posting of signs in their places of residence warning the neighbourhood of their presence. Here again there is a clash between the rights of the offender and the rights of children to protection.

Ofelia Calcetas-Santos

A role for UNESCO

Although the penal dimension is indispensable for clear enunciation of the criminal nature of the act committed by the paedophile and for dissuading and, where necessary, neutralizing him, it only operates within very narrow limits. Notwithstanding its unquestionably antisocial nature, paedophilia is a fact about which every society has 'unwittingly' created walls of silence. It is vital to stress the point that paedophilia forms part of a paedophilic fact which has found refuge in the walls of silence built by social structures confronted with sexual violence against children. Walls of silence behind which paedophilia, but not exclusively paedophilia by any means, can find favourable conditions for self-perpetuation. Could this perhaps be where UNESCO should concentrate its action?

The Convention on the Rights of the Child adopted in 1990 by the United Nations General Assembly has been ratified by 191 countries. This is a comprehensive and binding document. It covers all the rights of the child: civil, political, economic, social and cultural. We all know that the last two points are only the subject of a consensus and that their implementation poses many difficulties and may even considerably limit the scope and implementation of the Convention itself. It is, indeed, with regard to that statement that the participation of an organization such as UNESCO is particularly valuable because its spheres of competence include education and culture.

> States Parties undertake to protect the child from all forms of sexual exploitation and sexual abuse . . . [and] shall in particular take all appropriate national, bilateral and multilateral measures to prevent . . . the exploitative use of children in prostitution or other unlawful sexual practices . . . . Article 34, United Nations Convention on the Rights of the Child.

This is true with regard to maltreatment in the broadest sense. For example, in the particularly dramatic context of situations of war, extreme poverty, massive and forced population displacements where all forms of sexual abuse against children are commonplace, certain aggressors even dare to boast about this in the name of so-called ethnic purity or the perversion of certain ideologies.

The same applies to the dehumanizing value that certain precepts and conducts affecting children's bodies can have and also holds true, though on a more singular scale, in situations were the child is subject to paedophilic acts, whose staggering effects on the child's psyche can never be overstated. The situation is further magnified where there is violation of the body, a radically incomprehensible act for the child, particularly as, in the majority of cases, the aggressor is either a family member or well known to the child.

At this 'local' level, the child may encounter other types of silence: from his parents struck deaf and blind, from his peers or adult caretakers, from the judicial system too eager to ferret out 'proof' or so overburdened with reported cases that it can barely treat them. This silence can also, however, be found in non-respect of the conditions of neutrality needed to empower the child to evoke in any way at all the trauma which he has suffered. The present climate, which advocates precipitating revelation no matter what the cost, could be internalized by the child as a signal to keep quiet. In this regard, although it is important to give the child the right to speak, it is even more useful to allow the child the opportunity to be heard in as neutral a context as possible. That UNESCO should undertake to promote the respect for this requirement, over and above specific interests that may be raised in objection, seems to me to be in keeping with its mission to educate, which, quite naturally, involves taking account of underlying cultural diversity.

With regard to the paedophile, it is essential that he not be reduced to the sole dimension of his act, which does not exclude the penal dimension. This requires that due attention be paid to the very different aspects that the paedophile symptomatology presents. The latter cannot be contained in the one-dimensional picture presented by some media and whose unconsidered use will only lead to silencing other issues, which in various ways, and in the social context, also contribute to the mutism surrounding the fact of pae-dophilia. One need only remember the silence which until very recently shrouded these matters. A lot of work remains to be done if we are to under-stand who could, so effectively, have imposed such silence.

Chapter 9

PAEDOPHILIA: THE WORK OF ASSOCIATIONS AND THE ROLE OF THE MEDIA AND RESEARCH

Elisabeth Auclaire

Hardly a day goes by without another paedophilia case being reported in the media. One might get the impression that this evil is spreading at a dizzying pace. The time has come to take stock and reflect together on how to deal with the rise of uncontrolled emotion that we see every day, emotion that can contribute to creating a climate of aggression – with the potential to lead to lynchings – and that is conducive to the rise of extremist attitudes.

We have, therefore, seen the emergence of associations that, to protect passive 'child targets', launch petitions calling for increased repression and legislation, thereby – all too often – indiscriminately lumping together the causes, forms and consequences of violence against children.

The United Nations Convention on the Rights of the Child (UNCRC) clearly sets out the responsibilities of adults towards children, their own and all others, and also states that the rights of the child are not dissociable from human rights. The Convention considers these rights from the point of the view of the best interests of the child, recognized as a holder of vested rights.

The right to privacy, respect for one's private life and one's body *inter alia,* form part of the primordial rights that make up our freedom. Reflecting on these issues, and discussing them at our meetings with both adults and children means sharing our thoughts and ideas with all those involved in child development and contributing the skills and competences of experts who, in the field, try to rebuild these damaged lives.

Using the Internet for crimes against children makes them twice victims, the first time when they are actually abused, the second time when this abuse is seen by thousands or millions, and forever on the screen. We should use new information technology to educate and protect children, *not* to give them over to degenerate crimes. Jacques Danois, representative of Her Royal Highness Princess Caroline of Hanover.

Today the debate is being relaunched regarding the growth of paedophile networks on the Internet. The focus seems essentially to be on the exploitative aspect in the mercantile sense of the word. By concentrating on this very specific aspect of sexual abuse of children, we run the risk of relegating to a secondary position its most hidden, and by far most frequent, form, namely acts perpetrated within the family circle, by parents, grandparents, relatives, friends and acquaintances (nearly 80 per cent of child sexual abuse). Such acts are perpetrated by adults whom the child has learned to respect and obey. This, therefore, forces us to reflect on the underlying reasons, specify the terms we use and state their meanings clearly, and work with parents of young children and all those involved in raising and educating children from their youngest age, to provide them with sound information and guidance.

What can one say about paedophilia in the context of paedophile networks or prostitution? This most often occurs against the backdrop of extreme poverty and ignorance. Here again, one needs to combat the sources, the roots of these wretched and tragic stories. Stories that are interwoven with each country and with families, the environment, the economic situation, sources of income, educational structures and access to schooling and training.

Should we dwell excessively on the dangers of the Internet? After having made a scapegoat of television, blaming it for all violence, thus relieving ourselves of our responsibility as adults and parents, are we now going to make the Internet the latest scapegoat? Sources are at best extremely vague and few in number. It is apparently quite difficult, particularly for a child, to access such sites, let alone communicate with their managers. Tracking down these sites is the work of national law enforcement agencies and Interpol. It also goes without saying that if a net user accidentally comes across such a site, that person has a duty to inform the competent authorities.

We believe that our role lies elsewhere. Before calling for new laws, it would be advisable to review the battery of existing laws – which is fairly satisfactory – and urge more rigorous implementation, where necessary. Atrocious events of this kind have existed since the beginning of time. What family has not had its skeletons in the cupboard? The difference today, happily, is that we talk about them. We could, however, talk about them in ways that are less devastating for reflection and more constructive for children. It is incumbent on us to find new ways of talking about them.

Care must be taken not to make accusations without proof and not to see paedophiles around every corner. True vigilance means being responsive and genuinely attentive to the needs of others. More than protecting them, our duty is to help our children, to give them the means of defending themselves, and give them pointers for distinguishing a 'normal' and desirable display of affection and protectiveness by an adult towards a child from a more ambiguous attitude, which often causes discomfort in the child for reasons that he/she is not always able to identify. How can we inform our children without making them paranoid? At the rate we are going, the whole of society is on the verge of paranoia. How can we prevent everyone and everything from becoming suspect? Within the framework of the Committee on the Rights of the Child of the League for Human Rights, which was established in 1987 and has worked on a daily basis since then to defend the rights of children, these are some of the questions that we have been considering along with those active in the field and which we would like to open for further discussion.

Indeed, UNESCO does have a role to play in the thinking about the content and modes of dissemination of information and in the setting up of preventive education programmes. Children also need to be made aware that they have the right to say 'No', even to daddy or mummy, to family members, or, in some instances, to friends. Father does not always know best!

UNESCO, because of what it represents and through its impact in the world, can contribute to putting in place information and education systems with the appropriate partners according to the situation in each country. Rather than be afraid of paedophile networks on the Internet, why not use the Internet to counter their potential influence through outreach information campaigns aimed at families, parents of young children and children themselves, on the precautions to be taken when surfing a highway full of unknowns and through reminders of the law and the risks incurred by transgressors?

Suggestions for a preventive approach: adjusting national legislation

UNCRC signatory countries should adjust their legislation in line with the Convention.

Creating mediation spaces: These should be sufficiently neutral to ensure that the immediate response to the situation of abuse is not bureaucratically or institutionally driven. In every country there is a need for receptive places to which children can go without fear, sure of finding an attentive ear and effective assistance.

Setting up 'thinking' rather than 'doing' spaces: Because of the 'fragility' of children, their words can only be properly voiced in a neutral setting where confidentiality is guaranteed. The purpose of this confidentiality is not to counter what is reported but to respect the child's 'local scale'. The child must be able to talk about a difficult subject without immediately seeing his/her close environment threatened. These neutral spaces could be created in the child's public environment, particularly in schools wherever possible, without being subject to institutional authority.

A public health policy: There is a need for a comprehensive approach to the complexity of the causes of abuse. It is essential that the problems of abuse be dealt with entirely under the umbrella of public health. This is the only means of making such an approach possible.

What of research? Research in this field is essential, in order to ensure that a climate of 'witch hunts' does not take hold. It should be carried out in various fields, encompassing 'health', 'education' and 'information'. It should cover the various modes of communication transmission and be looked at from several angles.

Information and education: It is important to select the different types of messages and the means of communicating and evaluating them.

The media: The handling of subjects dealing with families and sexual abuse in the media should be observed. Representation and reception: do the stories feed fears or do they contribute to the useful and necessary clarification of facts that have for too long been hidden? With respect to the presence of child victims in television shows, we need to reflect on whether under the guise of first-hand accounts we are not, in fact, pandering to the voyeurism of viewers to the detriment of the real interests of the child who goes from being a subject to becoming an 'object'. The interim conclusion, like all conclusions, is that there is no 'one truth', but only child victims, generally suffering from feelings of guilt, who need to be helped to rebuild their personalities and first and foremost to shed these guilt feelings. We must bear in mind that in the not-so-distant, and perhaps not entirely forgotten, past, a young girl who had been raped was called a 'bitch' and a 'whore' by her own family. She was, in this way, doubly victimized. We should also reflect on the conditions under which reports are made. In defending human rights and the rights of the child, we must also remember that the right to dignity, to the presumption of innocence and to a fair trial, are shared rights that are equal for all.

CHILD PORNOGRAPHY, PAEDOPHILIA AND THE INTERNET

The Internet is a worldwide network of smaller computer networks and individual computers all connected by cable, telephone lines or satellite links. It is thus a decentralized, global medium of communication that links people around the world. No single entity administers it, nor is it located anywhere. It is timeless and spaceless. There is no single point at which all the information is stored or from which it is disseminated, and it is said that it would be not be technically feasible for any one entity to control all of the information conveyed therein.

> The analysis of Internet issues and the response to them is best understood against a backdrop of knowing its basic technology and the services it provides. Essentially, the Internet is a 'network of networks', of computers linked together using a series of protocols or rules which for all *practical* purposes represents a common language. From *Illegal and Harmful Use of the Internet*, Department of Justice, Equality and Law Reform, Dublin July 1998.

It is virtually impossible to determine the size of the Internet at any given moment. It has grown massively since its origins in 1969 as an experimental project to link research establishments. In 1981, fewer than 300 computers were connected to the Internet, but by 1996 over 9,400,000 host computers were estimated to be connected, 60 per cent of them in the United States. Reasonable estimates suggest that as many as 40 million people around the world can, and do, access this enormously flexible interactive communication medium. This figure was expected to grow to 200 million in 1999.

Using an Internet account, either though an Internet service provider (ISP) or an online provider, such as America Online, Compuserve or Microsoft, one can connect to the Internet through the provider's 'gateway'.

Everything on the Internet is global. When one accesses an item on the Net, people everywhere in the world can also access it. Something published on the Net can by read by everyone, immediately and worldwide. This global aspect of the Internet is one of its best qualities – it offers worldwide communication in real time and at little cost. People can talk to others without regard to geographical borders and without the constraints imposed by the traditional national and international telecommunications carriers.

> The Orchid club was a group of sixteen male child sex abusers coming from several different countries united only by their paedophilia. Each of these men had a video camera attached to their screens which enabled them together to watch a girl of 10 years being sexually abused in real time. They could directly participate in the abuse while it was taking place by offering suggestions and encouragement to the abuser. These men are now all arrested and the Orchid Club gone, but they are a graphic reminder of the fact that time and space no longer have the relevance they had for earlier generations. Ron O'Grady, Chairman of ECPAT, opening address at the Child Pornography on the Internet Experts Meeting, Lyon.

WWW stands for 'World Wide Web'. When people talk about surfing the Internet, they are actually talking about surfing the Web. The Web is a section of the Internet where information is cross-linked to other related information, allowing one to jump from one Web 'site' to another. It is also rich in graphics and sound and with the introduction of new applications, the Web has become more interactive and increasingly loaded with multimedia content. The Web is the most popular and fastest growing feature of the Internet and accounts for more than 90 per cent of Internet usage.

Chapter 10

CHILD PORNOGRAPHY ON THE INTERNET

Ofelia Calcetas-Santos

Risks to Children

While the value of the Internet as an educational tool is recognized because of the wealth of information found therein – much of which is of value for developing countries – this same technological wonder can pose threats for children. One of these is child pornography, a disturbing phenomenon which has generated increasing concern about the Net in recent years.

There are two ways in which children can be potentially reached and harmed by child pornography on the Net: by being exposed to it as inadvertent viewers, or by themselves becoming the subject of films and photographs broadcast on the Net. Child pornography to which children can be exposed may take the form of text, pictures or communications via Internet relay 'chat rooms'. It is carried on bulletin boards, in newsgroups and other forms of Internet communication. It extends from the mildly titillating what is mildly titillating child pornography. However, this could lead some young minds to the conclusion that if it is on the screen, then it must be OK.

> A major concern is the ease with which pornographic material can be accessed, stored and disseminated on the Internet. There is a strong perception that the Internet has become a major factor in the development of paedophile rings worldwide and many recent convictions in the United States and in the United Kingdom have shown that the medium is being widely used by members of such rings, both to share experience and *to* traffic in child pornographic images. From *Illegal and Harmful Use of the Internet*, Department of Justice, Equality and Law Reform, Dublin, July 1998.

IRC (Internet relay chat) 'chat rooms' are particularly threatening, allowing the user to hide behind a false identity and/or age. Thus, a child might be easily tempted to give real personal details which could in turn lead to exploitative situations through actual involvement in prostitution and/or pornography.

Where a child is filmed or photographed in a sexually explicit manner, he or she is by definition being subjected to the grossest violation of his or her human rights. Every pornographic photograph or videotape becomes a permanent record of that child's abuse.

The dissemination of child pornography over the Internet is reportedly becoming prolific over web pages, bulletin boards and newsgroup servers. Images of children, sometimes as young as eight or nine, depicting their rape, torture and even murder, can be downloaded easily by anyone with basic knowledge of the Internet.

This global computer communications network has also become the latest vehicle for trafficking in women and children. It is widely used by men to exchange detailed information on where to find children for sex, or to give information on actual locations where pimps sell pre-teen girls, the sex acts that can be bought, and the price for each act.

Surveys carried out done by on-line administrators suggest that pornographic sites in general are among those most often visited on the Internet. Determining the percentage of users of child pornography is more difficult as very often this material is included with adult pornography, or is protected by encryption devices that make detection very difficult. It is not surprising that pornographers and other promoters of sexual exploitation tend to be experts in the technical means of ensuring privacy and anonymity.

Why the Internet?

The Internet is a very attractive place for producers and consumers of child pornography for a number of reasons. Firstly, the technology makes constant updating very easy – some services claim to update their material biweekly. Secondly, it reaches a global audience faster than any other media. Thirdly, it provides digital-quality images at far less expense than the paper catalogues that used to be the common medium. Fourthly, pictures and film clips can be downloaded into the computer and have the advantage over film that their quality does not deteriorate with age or with transfer to another computer. Fifthly, those who distribute pornography seek security in the anonymity perceived to be offered by the Internet, enabling the user to invent virtually any identity and route a message through different countries in order to avoid detection.

The most advanced technology on the Internet is live video conferencing – live audio and video transmitted over the Internet from a video camera and microphone to a computer. This development has raised child pornography to an even higher level, giving the impact of three-dimensional virtual reality and enabling the viewer to participate interactively and give orders on how the scene should be played.

> States Parties shall ensure that no child shall be subjected to torture or other cruel, inhuman or degrading treatment or punishment. Neither capital punishment nor life imprisonment without possibility of release shall be imposed for offences committed by persons below 18 years of age. . . . Article 37, United Nations Convention on the Rights of the Child.

The only limitation to this type of global sex show is the need for high speed transmission, processing and multimedia capabilities. As more users gain access to high-speed multimedia computer and transmission equipment, this type of private sex show will grow – a person may be on one continent while directing and watching a live pornographic show involving children in another.

Purposes and uses of child pornography

Producers and/or senders of child pornography are suppliers meeting a demand. This naturally leads to advertising – of the availability of the children used in the making of the pornographic material, in the form of catalogues showing pictures of the children and listing their ages, nationalities, physical attributes and sexual preferences.

Users or viewers of child pornography – including paedophiles – may use it as a form of escapism or fantasy, and for them the pornography is an end unto itself, leading no further than masturbation. There are those, however, for whom viewing child pornography serves to stimulate sexual desire as a prelude to actual sexual activity with children.

Child pornography can be used by exploiters to lower children's inhibitions in order to seduce or encourage them to freely participate either in prostitution or pornography. Paedophiles and child abusers also use pornography to legitimize their actions and to convince themselves that their behaviour is not abnormal, but is shared by others.

Child pornography can also be used as a medium of exchange with other exploiters in public and private sex markets. Sexually explicit images of children may be used to blackmail the child victims into obedience or silence. There is evidence that child pornography is being used as an active tool by homosexuals for the recruitment of young boys.

Although money is usually not the primary concern of users, it can be very profitable for the producers. Hard-core pornographic material is encrypted and the producers sell the key to the code for a fee.

The production and dissemination of pornographic material are used to desensitize society in general, and to send a message that children are legitimate sex partners. This is a very insidious strategy, as it renders the general public inured to the presence of children in pornography and lessens any indignation they would normally otherwise feel under ordinary circumstances.

Chapter 11

RESEARCH, INFORMATION AND SENSITIZING THE PUBLIC

Ulla Carlsson

Our cultures are currently experiencing a new phase in the process of the digitization of communication. Technology is changing the options available to media audiences, and we are expected, and able, to choose what we consume to a far greater extent. Consider, for example, that only twenty years ago viewers in Sweden had access to only two national channels. One consequence of this proliferation of channels and sources of information and culture is a fragmentation and individualization of the audience. Our shared experience of mass media is shrinking, which means that our common frame of reference concerning society around us is weakened. The Internet is generally singled out as the most striking illustration of the 'digital revolution'. The Internet is now making the transition into a new phase – from being considered merely as a technology to representing a medium of information and communication. More and more, the accessibility of the Internet grows, and it is a medium that is not schedule-bound, but which consists of a continuous flow. In many respects, the Internet is a medium for the young.

It is evident to us at the UNESCO International Clearing House on Children and Violence on the Screen that violent content has found its way onto the 'Net', and it is relatively easy to gain access to this material. The violence is both fictional and documentary. Thus, the Internet is yet another channel of communication through which we can be exposed to gratuitous violence; clearly, the violent content available there must be studied on a par with the output of other media. This is a new task for media scholars.

> The Internet readily facilitates the storage and transmission of two other forms of child pornography: text-based material and audio-pornography. Today, the

> Internet is increasingly used by paedophiles to exchange graphic correspondence and to exchange knowledge and experiences. Audio-pornography can be stored in digital files for transmission over electronic mail, displayed on a www site or can be posted to a newsgroup. From *Illegal and Harmful Use of the Internet*, Department of Justice, Equality and Law Reform, Dublin, July 1998.

We also note the increasing presence of violence of another kind on satellite television channels and on the Internet. I am referring to the violence in pornographic films and images. Professor Jo Groebel has shown how easy it is to access sadistic pornography on the Internet, particularly via newsgroups. The kinds of violence perpetrated against women in this content are an important component in the social structures which portray women as inferior to men. These kinds of violence require somewhat different approaches and methods of analysis than have generally been applied in traditional studies of media violence. Media researchers have not focused to any appreciable extent on such content and the issues it raises. We have seen remarkably few studies of the effects of pornography on those who view it, and we know even less about the effects on young, and very young, viewers. Studies of sadistic pornography are even rarer. However, the possibility that violent pornography may lead some men to commit rape is widely debated in many societies today.

In this connection it is also important to point out that we know hardly anything about how media depictions of sex influence children. Content analyses tell us, however, that sex scenes are much more common on television today than they were only a decade or so ago. How might this influence young viewers' attitudes, values and behaviour? We should have the benefit of answers to this question when we set about studying the effects of viewing pornography.

The issue of pornography on the Internet automatically leads us to the issue of child pornography on the net. Both the distribution and possession of child pornography are criminal offences in most countries today. The problem has aroused considerable attention in recent years, both in media coverage and among law enforcement authorities. Effective cooperation between national police forces aims to track down and arrest offenders, but also to monitor media content. In addition, some major organizations such as the European Union and ECPAT have also taken initiatives. Finally, a mass movement is being mobilized at different levels in the world community to combat sexual exploitation of minors, child pornography and paedophilia on the Internet.

That the Internet is used to distribute child pornography is indisputable. The Net is used not just to reproduce and disseminate child pornography, but also as a vehicle for soliciting and procuring. The rapidity, economy and simplicity of the medium has expanded the distribution of child pornography immensely. The Net's global reach implies unprecedented potential for effectively spreading illegal images. At the same time, we should bear in mind that the Internet comprises several different elements including the World Wide Web, Usenet and IRC (Internet relay chat). Arrests have been made and material confiscated, mainly in newsgroups on Usenet. Self-regulation seems to have been more effective where websites are concerned.

Child pornography on the Internet has proved far more elusive than other pornographic material. Given that child pornography is almost universally socially unacceptable and illegal, preserving one's anonymity is of prime interest among those who exchange illegal matter via the Net. Nonetheless, any reasonably skilled Internet user can find child pornographic content.

To the extent that the Internet serves as a medium of mass communication, mass communication researchers have major tasks. They can analyse the content and determine its effects on users – adults and children alike. But they should also explore the possibilities for the information society, via self-regulation, to come to terms with a new media landscape. Conceivably, unless dealt with effectively, the presence of child pornography on the Net may call into question the legitimacy of free, uncontrolled flows of information – the *raison d'être* of the Internet itself.

Research on child pornography on Internet – a larger complex

Even so, the problem which UNESCO must address is considerably broader than all this. It might be formulated thus: what role does the presence and accessibility of child pornography on the Internet play with respect to the problem of sexual exploitation and sexual abuse of children in the world today? The problem we face is far more extensive and more serious: the possibility that child pornography on the Internet may lead to more widespread sexual exploitation of minors. Addressing this problem will require the commitment and collaboration of many different disciplines and professions: psychology, sociology, criminology, law, political science, religion, philosophy and so forth. Media researchers are but one – in this context perhaps even peripheral – discipline among many that can contribute to casting light on and combating so complex a problem as the sexual abuse of children.

Something discussed on the periphery of public debate is the possibility of adverse effects on young Internet users who come in contact with illegal material and the question of effects on adults. It is in relation to questions like these that mass communication researchers can, together with psychologists and criminologists, provide new insights. A number of aspects must be taken into account – cognitive, emotional, attitudinal, behavioural and so on. Systematic studies that apply a battery of methods are called for: laboratory experiments, observations and surveys, followed by more comprehensive longitudinal studies. A first, decisive question is how this kind of research can best be facilitated. So far, conditions have not been ideal. UNESCO, with its wealth of experience in scientific research, would seem well equipped to initiate highly relevant multinational and multidisciplinary research projects.

> Children's problems are so serious that no government is capable of solving them; therefore, it requires a cooperation from all sectors of society. Ofelia Calcetas Santos, UN Special Rapporteur on Special Rapporteur on the Sale of Children, Sexual Exploitation of Children and Child Pornography during her official visit to Guatemala, July-August 1999.

However, before we can study the effects of pornography, sadistic pornography and child pornography, we need to know more about what is available – its accessibility and content – and how many and which people consume it, as well as the circumstances under which they do so. Studies of this nature have been few and far between to date.

We at the International Clearing House will naturally do everything we can to stimulate research and to make research findings known, so as to increase our collective and cumulative knowledge of how children and young people use, and are affected by viewing, sadistic pornography and child pornography. Ultimately, it is a question of safeguarding children's rights, and in this work we are guided by Article 17 of the Convention on the Rights of the Child which enjoins us to ensure children's access to information and material of social and cultural benefit to them, while protecting them from material that is harmful to their well-being.

Chapter 12

PAEDOPHILES NETWORKING ON THE INTERNET

Rachel O'Connell

Introduction

The broad array of communication channels provided by the Internet facilitates the creation of many diverse communities. This chapter is concerned with how individuals dedicated to child sex organize themselves within what can be best described as virtual communities or networks, i.e., community structures and roles held by individuals who never meet in person, and where anonymous interaction is based solely on various forums of Internet activity. The Internet provides a uniquely safe, easily accessible, distribution medium that operates on at least three levels simultaneously.

First, the technology facilitates the anonymous, rapid dissemination of an immediate and constant supply of illegal child pornography pictures, i.e., a virtual stream of sexualized child fantasy depictions. For adults with a sexual interest in children it facilitates the expression of their fantasies for the purposes of affirmation. These images are posted in a sympathetic environment that is supportive of their rationalizations for child sex encounters.

Second, it enables creation and maintenance of a sense of deviant behaviour. The presence of complex social structures in the computer underground indicates that on a social organizational level, adults with a sexual interest in children act as 'colleagues'. They devise ways of preventing discovery, apprehension and sanctioning by social control agents. This knowledge is also anonymously disseminated transnationally through the distribution medium of the Internet.

Third, the Internet provides a facilitating and supportive context. The easy accessibility and transnational distribution of child pornography and the rationalizations for child sex have broader implications in the context of sexualizing children to an audience who may not have any primary interest in child sex *per se*. The children depicted in child pornography images are engaged in sexual behaviour, and are directed by the photographer to behave in specific ways that serve to sexualize children in order to gratify a whole range of fantasies. The result is that the children engaged in sex acts are often smiling or have neutral expressions, and very rarely do children in child pornographic pictures show signs of discomfort. These depictions appear to be designed to reinforce rationalization and justification processes for adult sexual interest in children. To the wider audience the pictures depict children as 'willing sexual beings'. Given this, issues concerning the 'rights of the child' and indeed the nature of childhood are continually moving further and further into the background.

The focus of this chapter is Usenet newsgroups dedicated to child sex as the most obvious medium in the dissemination of child pornography, and on the most visible evidence of paedophile networking on the Internet. Newsgroups provide a passive supportive, virtual environment that facilitates the discussion of fantasies and alleged experiences of sexual offences against children in a context which routinizes, sanitizes and normalizes sexual contact with children.

The most visible and distinctive feature of paedophile activity on the Internet is trading in child erotica and child pornographic pictures. Usenet facilitates the formation of what could be called a virtual deviant market, involving complex networks of users for trade that is effectively anonymous. Deviant exchange is voluntary; participants have compatible interests and cooperate in satisfying those interests.

Newsgroups are only one outlet for the expression of adult sexual interest in children on the Internet. Newsgroups provide a very public form of virtual communication; other communication protocols enable real time private communication, and it is reasonable to suppose that they have a greater role in the passage of direct sensitive information, as well as supporting the distribution of pornography. It is likely that protocols such as email, 'I seek you' (ICQ) and Internet relay chat (IRC) have a greater role than newsgroups in the dissemination of 'private' photographs, and are vehicles for information related to contacts.

This chapter also addresses the content of child erotic and child pornographic pictures posted in child-sex-related newsgroups. The analysis of content may be viewed from at least two perspectives:

> First, child pornography is the evidence of serious sexual assaults on children. The pictures may reveal a wealth of information from an operational policing perspective in circumstances where child protection issues are concerned. How-

ever, the vast majority of photographs found in newsgroups involve youths aged 15 to 20 years old and therefore do not raise immediate issues of child protection. The identification of new from old is therefore an important issue that may have a direct child protection value. The evidential nature of child pornography is a subject that has been explored by the COPINE team and especially by one of the COPINE partners, the Paedophilia Unit of the Metropolitan Police Service, London. As evidence, child pornography pictures are amenable to crime scene analysis and have a role in revealing the identity of the child and very occasionally the identity of the offender.

Second, the nature of the fantasies contained in child pornography may also be indicative of the qualities of the picture collector from a psychological, and potentially an offending, perspective. The sense in which pictures can be analysed from this perspective is addressed in this chapter.

There are two assumptions being made here: first, that pornographic depictions are representative of desired fantasies which is one of the principle reasons why they are collected; second, within the context of the Internet the pictures a user posts are representative of that particular individual's fantasies and sexual predilections. There is a lack of psychological research with regard to both of these assumptions, and a working through of these issues is one major area of research that the COPINE project seeks to address.

A potential caveat to the above, as far as newsgroup postings are concerned, is that the pictures may not in fact necessarily always reflect the kind of pictures that an individual would choose to best cater for his or her personal fantasies in relation to child sex. The dynamics of posting may have a range of purposes outside of meeting particular fantasies, that are related to the social context of the virtual network in which an individual is involved. The purpose of posting may be any or all of the following:

- to sustain and legitimize through participation, deviant sexual interest in children;
- to gain credence amongst the members of a virtual community or network by posting pictures that cater to a number of different fantasies;
- to help others in completing series of pictures, therefore posting pictures again outside of personal tastes, to gain both status and in the hope of 'quid pro quo' posting that better reflects personal tastes;
- to simply engage in the process of collecting for its own sake;
- to explore deviant forms of sexuality, including but not exclusively adult sexual interest in children.

However, of even greater significance would be knowledge of the relationship between collection of child pornography and the potential to sexually assault children. Are there within collections of child pornography indications of potential 'dangerousness' of collectors, in terms of sexual assaults on children?

Perhaps the most significant factor influencing the growth of child pornography on the Internet is the ease of dissemination and collection. Such anonymity and convenience, eliminating the need to expose identity in a transaction, has revealed quite an extraordinary level of adult sexual interest in children. Presumably this interest was either dormant or latent on this scale in the past.

The Internet Allows Paedophiles:
- Instant access to other predators worldwide;
- Open discussion of their sexual desires;
- Shared ideas about ways to lure victims;
- Mutual support of their adult-child sex philosophies;
- Instant access to potential child victims worldwide;
- Disguised identities for approaching children, even to the point of presenting oneself as a member of teen groups;
- Ready access to 'teen chat rooms' to find out how and who to target as potential victims;
- Means to identify and track down home contact information;
- Ability to build a long-term 'Internet' relationship with a potential victim, prior to attempting to engage the child in physical contact.

Adapted from 'Internet Pedophile Overview', Dr Nancy Faulkner and Debbie Mahoney, SOC-UM (http://www.soc-um.org/online.html), quoted with permission.

The advent of the Internet has meant that child pornography is far more accessible and available to those with even minimal computer skills. Therefore the dynamics of producing, collecting, trading and distributing child pornography have been transformed. In addition, the scope for selection of particular pictures that cater for specific desires has also increased.

Analysis of newsgroup posters' activity reflects only those persons who decide to actively engage in the process of posting. Experience suggests that there are many users who simply 'lurk' in the background and download the pictures they require. Therefore a 'hidden layer of activity' exists, the extent, size and number of participants of which is unknown.

As noted above, 'hidden markets' may also be operating through the less public medium of private email. 'Email' lists expand email from 'one-to-one' to 'one-to-many' recipients, facilitating the creation of private information or discussion groups. The 'Ianthe'-based support group for 'girl lovers' is an example of this. Other communication protocols afford parallel or complementary means of communication, which offer additional levels of anonymity.

These include for example, Internet relay chat rooms which afford users the opportunity to communicate in 'real time' and most closely resemble an on-line 'conversation'. IRC also affords the option to open a Direct Channel of Communication (DCC) between two users, which bypasses the need for a server and thereby raises the level of security of the communications.

IRC historically was a major forum for the exchange of child pornography, and there is clear evidence of its use to organize and orchestrate the sexual abuse of children as well as to propagate the trade in child pornography. Some IRC users formed close and complex social networks to facilitate and control both the exchange of photographs and information. A similar protocol such as 'I Seek You' (abbreviated as 'ICQ') has the advantage of operating in the form of a pager system. Again, the extent of this activity is at present largely unknown.

A central factor relates to the distributed nature of the Internet and its facilitation of anonymity. This allows users to adopt any number of pseudo personalities to explore both deviant and non-deviant roles. The term 'multisex deviants' has been coined to describe Usenet users for whom an interest in child sex is a part of a larger circle of deviant sexual interests. The significance of fantasy noted earlier again becomes relevant here. The critical problem is untangling fantasy from reality and understanding how they relate.

The analysis of the content of pictures posted in child sex related newsgroups suggests that individual posters are indeed highly specific and selective in the kinds of pictures that they post. This selectivity and specificity can be defined in terms of a number of factors including: sex of the child; stage of development of the child; ethnic origin of child; sexual interaction; use of force; adult involvement; sex of adult; number of adults; ethnic origin of adults; and sexual behaviour. Our analysis suggests that there are indeed indications of individuals' sexual preferences in these depictions.

Of particular interest is the notion that individuals can express various kinds of sexual preferences, and that these preferences may be made up of quite dissimilar elements. Knowledge of deviant sexual interest, however, is difficult to obtain. Convicted offenders provide the most accessible source of research. An underlying assumption of studies involving offenders (who can be reached for questioning) is that convicted offenders in some sense reflect the broader population of non-convicted offenders. Surveys have, for example, found that some offenders have assaulted many child victims and that a proportion are also involved in committing other sexually deviant acts such as rape of female adults.

The majority of these studies have examined group differences (child molesters vs. non-child sex molesters) to evaluate the presence of inappropriate sexual age preferences. Although the results are consistent, not all child molesters show the same response profile. As a group, child molesters sometimes respond in a bimodal fashion, that is to say some may respond maximally to prepubescent children and adults and less to adolescents. The Internet provides an opportunity to further explore issues such as this among what might be termed as the more 'normal' population. The following describes an initial study of fantasy qualities of child pornography that is being conducted within a specific evidential framework.

STUDY 1: Structure and social organization of paedophile newsgroup activity

From an analysis of paedophile activity in Usenet newsgroups it is possible to describe the structure and social organization of paedophile activity. Posters to paedophile newsgroups can be identified as having a variety of roles, some of which might be termed 'promoting', i.e., promoting the paedophile stance, and others 'detracting', i.e., detracting from the paedophile stance. The main 'promoting' roles are described below.

Promoters

Infrastructure advice/coordinators: These people act as a protective buffer zone orchestrating paedophile Usenet newsgroup activity and give advice about the most appropriate way to respond to 'Flames' (anti-paedophile reactionaries) in the following ways: writing Frequently Asked Questions (FAQ) texts to help child-sex-related newsgroup readers, especially new readers, in the group by preempting and answering any questions they might have about the group and how it operates; providing technical information about how to download and decode articles; giving advice about how to post anonymously by using anonymous remailers; making posts that are encouraging and supportive; and giving email addresses of the authors that afford new users the opportunity to comment directly to the authors via private correspondence, i.e., email.

'Infrastructure advice coordinators' also give advice on which newsgroups are best to post articles to, particularly those articles that contain pictures. In this way they orchestrate the migratory pattern of newsgroup posters. An example of this can be seen in an excerpt from an infrastructure advice coordinator's posting: 'Posting pictures of nudity is allowed, although you might want to consider posting them to (a particular newsgroup whose name includes the word nudism) and posting a note here. If you post such a picture here, make sure you put "nude" in the subject line.'

The important point to highlight here is that integrating oneself into a virtual paedophile community or network is not signposted in any traditional manner but virtual rules and 'netiquette' do very definitely exist. These infrastructure advice coordinators would generally be the first line of contact for any 'newbie' (new participant) to the virtual paedophile world. They are the purveyors of the rules of conduct and seem only too pleased to adopt a hospitable role in outlining the various points of 'netiquette' that are imperatives to navigating successfully in the paedophile world. These people play a central role in the deviant process, although it may not always be clear whether they are committing an offence.

Literature reviewers: These people give detailed information regarding the content of paedophile-related publications – books and magazines – and how to procure these items. They also give details about how to become a member of paedophile organisations and the addresses of paedophile websites. The following is an excerpt from a literature reviewer's post: 'Acolyte Reader Series. In the long running Acolyte Reader Series, the short story format allows for an impressive variety in each volume. . . . Bob Henderson's warmly romantic piece demonstrates why it is so hard for some men to stop loving boys: there are just too many of them waiting to be loved.'

Story/fantasy generators: These web pages directly engage in the production of fantasy material, by posting stories containing lurid accounts of sexual interactions between adults and children. It is impossible to know if these are real or fantasy accounts of personal experience, although some are so bizarre as to strain anyone's belief.

Support people: The main role of these posters is to contribute to the non-threatening, facilitating and supportive context in which sexual interest in children can develop. They detail positive aspects of adult-child sexual interaction, claim to disagree with coerced sex between adults and children and fully support consensual sex between adults and children. The following example of the content of a support person's posting is taken from a thread entitled 'Why does sexual contact harm children? Anyone with any degree of sensitivity has to be concerned about the physical, emotional and sexual "child abuse" that exists in today's society. But this does not imply that all relationships between youth and adults are exploitative and abusive. One merely has to read what others have posted to this group and elsewhere regarding their own positive experiences when they were young'.

A particular feature of these postings is the support of the rights of 'boy' and 'girl' lovers, and the drawing of a distinction between paedophiles and child molesters.

Posters and traders of child erotic and child pornographic pictures: Those who actually engage in posting pictures are generally quite specific in what they do. Such posters may fall into the following categories: child erotica only; child pornographic only; hard-core child pornography only; mixed child erotica and child pornography; multi-sex deviants, i.e., people who post articles in newsgroups about multiple forms of adult sex, fetishes, bestiality, sadomasochism, child pornography and child erotica. Their interest in child erotica and child pornography seems to figure as part of an insatiable interest in multiple sexual deviant fantasies.

It is very difficult to assess whether the poster of what appears to be a 'recent picture' was in fact the producer of that picture. This is due in part to the inordinately rapid communication protocols that make up the Internet. A hypothetical example will illustrate this as follows: A series of 'new pictures' is posted by one paedophile – a section of this series may be posted by another paedophile shortly afterwards as 'my favourite picture'. A short while later, perhaps the same day, another paedophile may post the section of the series he had access to and ask for 'fills', i.e., the remaining pictures in the series. Each of these posters could be from different continents, so that within a single day a number of different posters from different parts of the world have posted the sections of the same picture series. In 1996 a colleague traced the movement of a marked picture from Europe to North America, and the same picture from Australia to Europe, in the course of 24 hours. It is impossible for an investigator to be certain of who originally posted a picture, which country the pictures originated from, or of the relationship – if any – between the producer of the pictures and the posters. Once a picture enters the public domain it may subsequently be posted by a large number of people, and details such as the originator of a picture from its posting history easily become blurred.

Detractors

Reactionary: These posters react aggressively against the content of paedophile newsgroup postings, e.g., 'When the balloon goes up, I want first shot at this filthy bunch of child abusing scumbags'. Posters such as these appear frequently in child sex related newsgroups and reflect the level of repugnance that some people feel towards adults with a sexual interest in children.

Paedophile register propagators: Here is a sample using fictitious data:

> *Name:* J... S...
> *Sex:* Male
> *Weight:* 160 lbs.
> *Eyes:* Brown
> *DOB:* 10/11/57
> *Registration City:* Huntington
> *Registered State:* NY
> *Convicted:* 07/24/96
> *Charge:* Child seduction
> *Sentence:* 3 years w/1.5 years suspended.

This posting appears to be used to tempt someone to 'take out' a person with a conviction for child seduction.

A major role of the 'infrastructure advice coordinators', as noted above, is to advise participants to simply ignore these articles. Paradoxically it would appear that instead of discouraging paedophile activity on Usenet newsgroups, the anti-paedophile reactionaries might well serve to aid a process of group cohesiveness among paedophiles. By voicing a very real threat to their activities it would be reasonable to suggest that this accentuates a need among paedophiles for group cohesiveness and reinforces the important role of 'Infrastructure/advice Coordinators'. As with so many well-intentioned initiatives in this area (such as the anti-child pornography website) they actually encourage and develop paedophile activity on the Net, rather than diminish and control it.

Findings of Study 1

This study highlighted the following:

- The structure and social organization of paedophile networking activity on the Internet as outlined above does not appear to operate in a strictly hierarchical fashion. Instead, posters adopt a cooperative approach with an 'organizing executive', i.e., an 'Infrastructure advice coordinator';
- A large amount of the activity on picture-based child erotica and child pornography newsgroups is driven in a cooperative manner, around swapping pictures. Posts may ask for a certain picture to complete a particular series, or contain what are considered as 'prize pictures', 'recent pictures', or offers of free CDs of series of photos for all to access;
- A focus on completing a series of pictures by filling in missing pictures, and the frequency with which recent-looking pictures appear, gives an indication of the organized approach that these users adopt in relation to their child pornography collections and their appetite for newness;
- To sustain this activity it seems reasonable to assert that newness and novelty both play a crucial role in this process. The volume of material posted is enormous: in a two-week period in January 1998, a total of 6,034 child erotica and child pornography pictures were posted in child sex related newsgroups – and this figure does not take into account the number of pictures available on CDs. It is reasonable to expect that to sustain the interest of the newsgroup readers there would be a great need for new material.

STUDY 2: Identifying newsgroups posting child erotica and child pornography

The analyses sought to identify newsgroups in which child erotic and child pornographic pictures were posted. The method involved subscribing to a newsreader that provided access to all newsgroups in which pictures were posted. A full list of these newsgroups was printed and the names of newsgroups that suggested that they might be concerned with adult sexual interest in children were noted. These newsgroups were then accessed via a second archival database and the messages posted there were read by the researcher and any reference made to any other newsgroup in relation to adult sexual interest in children was also noted. Once the active newsgroups that contained child erotica and child pornographic pictures were identified, a detailed analysis of the pictures posted to these newsgroups in a one-week period was carried out.

A content analysis was then carried out of the pictures that each individual posted to each newsgroup, thereby gaining an insight into each individual's posts and also the overall distribution of pictures depicting child erotica and those depicting child pornography. The pseudonym of each poster was noted for purposes of checking for the same pseudonym appearing in both analyses. A crosscheck of the content of the postings made by individuals during both periods could be carried out to identify similarities or differences in the content of an individual's posts.

Newsgroups that contain female child erotica and pornographic pictures: In total 15 newsgroups were identified that contained female child erotica and pornographic pictures. The largest amount of picture posting took place in newsgroups that contained the words 'pre-teen' and 'children' in the title. The overall number of female child pictures posted in the period of analysis in January 1998 amounted to 3,487, posted by 193 users.

Male child newsgroups: The newsgroups where users posted male child erotica and pornography pictures were located. These generally contained the word 'boy' somewhere in the title. Over the last three years, there has been a clear movement of child pornography between 4 or 5 newsgroups.

Newsgroups that contain pictures of male and female children together: Newsgroups that contain pictures of both male and female children together were very few. These pictures were posted in both the male and female child newsgroups. Many of the pictures that contain both male and female children together are erotic in nature and seem to originate from nudist magazines. A small number of these pictures depict child to child sexual interaction. It is interesting to note that the number of pictures, and number of people posting pictures depicting both male and female children together are less than those depicting female children only or male children only. This suggests that individual posters are highly selective in the sex of the children depicted in the pictures they post.

Newsgroups that do not contain child erotic or pornographic pictures: Eight newsgroups were located whose names suggested that they would contain pictures of child erotica and pornography. But these newsgroups generally did not contain any such pictures. Before the systematic analysis of newsgroups was engaged in, the main newsgroup that contained pictures of female children carried in its title the word 'fucking'. The activity in this newsgroup subsequently moved to 'pre-teen' so the former is now defunct in terms of child pornography and contains instead adult pornography.

Paedophile newsgroups as a percentage of the total number of newsgroups: It is salutary to put in context the percentage of paedophile newsgroups dedicated to trading child erotica and child pornography pictures in relation to the total number of newsgroups. The total number of Usenet newsgroups that contain child erotica and pornography amounts to 0.07 per cent of the total number of newsgroups. Set in this context, the percentage of newsgroups dedicated to paedophile picture trading may seem quite small; yet from an organizational perspective, restricting their activities to a limited number of newsgroups has obvious advantages for the group. It does not in any way restrict the large amount of paedophile picture trading that takes place in this small number of newsgroups.

What do we learn if we analyse some of the content from some of the most active paedophile posters? It would be expected that a person who consistently posts a particular kind of picture depicting particular kinds of children involved in particular behaviours, might actually sexually prefer that type of person or behaviour.

Pseudonyms of posters: These pseudonyms represent some of the core set of posters addressing the pre-teen newsgroup. This suggests that the individuals behind these pseudonyms are aware of each other, and that there may be private communication between them. They constitute, in a very real way, a virtual paedophile network. All of this indicates that among paedophile picture posters an important social structure has developed, since maintaining the same pseudonym facilitates being identified as an active participant in the process. Presumably this facilitates gaining recognition for themselves (albeit virtual recognition) as the 'gurus' of this activity since they, it seems, have access to large numbers of pictures and post regularly.

The implication of identifying consistent posters is that it is possible to track particular paedophiles' activities within the newsgroups; of even more interest are their patterns of posting across time. Do they consistently post pictures depicting the same elements of fantasy? If they have been specific about certain elements of a fantasy (e.g., the sex of a child), does this change across time? Further analysis of newsgroup activity across time may give an indication of the effect of this virtual environment on particular paedophiles.

Findings of Study 2

These concerned:

- Segregation of the sexes. Paedophiles are highly selective in terms of the newsgroups in which they post pictures: pictures of girls are posted mainly in the newsgroup 'pre-teens', while those of boys pictures are posted in 'boys'.
- Two-thirds of the pictures posted could be described as erotic in nature and many appear to be relatively recent. Many feature children of Asian extraction or include text indicating Japanese origins. Taking erotic pictures of children presumably indicates a high demand in the market for the pro-

duction of child pornography (not withstanding its illegality in Japan). Pornographic photographs (as distinct from erotic) are largely either old European photographs, or more recent ones featuring Asian children;

- The form in which pictures are posted. The number of pictures posted refers to individual pictures, but very often these pictures form part of a series. Each series can number anything from one to 500. Each series may confine itself to depicting a single child centred on one theme, or many contain a number of children engaged in various different sex acts that progress in invasiveness as the series numbers ascend. Individual posters may post a section of a series that contains pictures that cater for their own specific fantasies. Alternatively, they may be missing certain images and they will post messages asking for 'fills' for the series, i.e., the missing images in a certain section. Posters also post recent-looking 'new pictures', which are posted to trade and made available to other news-group users;

- It seems likely that most of the pictures have their origins either in scanned magazine photographs, or in video captures. New erotic (as opposed to pornographic) photographs are mainly scanned from Japanese magazines. There are also growing numbers of digitized video clips, derived from videotape originals. In the absence of a systematic database of material it is not possible to judge the extent to which material is primarily produced for distribution on the Internet, as distinct from being a secondary product of other media. Our impression is that little, if any, of the child pornography currently accessible on newsgroups was produced originally in digital form. It seems likely that this will change in the future. We are currently engaged in a detailed analysis of postings to explore some of these issues further.

Conclusions

The findings of these studies suggest that adults with a sexual interest in child sex organize themselves with distinct social structures within a virtual community. The Internet provides an easily accessible, uniquely safe, supportive context for posting, trading and collecting illegal material such as child pornography. The multilayered and multifaceted nuances of the child-sex-related criminal underworld presents unique challenges to law enforcement and legislative bodies.

First and foremost is the illegality of child pornography, which needs to be considered within the context of a deviant market. The existence of such a large number of people engaged in accessing child-sex-related Internet sites clearly creates a market for pornography and information in general. This illegal material drives the market, which is distinctive in that it typically does not involve the exchange of money. That is not to say that money is not involved, for example, in the production of the very many magazines that seem to provide the bulk of the recent erotica found on the Internet. However, newsgroup activity suggests a huge leakage from that market into what is effectively a free service. Newsgroup activity seems to present an example of a complex criminal conspiracy *not* based on the exchange of money.

Two major kinds of involvement in the collection and distribution of child pornography on the Internet can be identified, i.e., those passively benefiting from these activities, as collectors; and those actively engaged in the process of trading pictures, information, and so forth.

Passive involvement in child pornography through browsing, downloading, etc., is very difficult to detect. There are an unknown number of people engaged in the passive monitoring and downloading of images and information, but all the evidence is that many people at least browse in this area, even if they not actively downloading. For example, the 'hit' rates to a well-known site for 'girl lovers' suggest that many thousands of people regularly review that page for information on girl-sex related sites. There is a sense, therefore, in which these people constitute a passive market for child pornography and erotica, and thereby fuel the process. The management and detection of these people presents major difficulties.

The second group identified above, those people 'actively' involved, in many ways constitutes the greater problem. These individuals, by actively distributing illegal photographs, are in a position analogous to that of a drug dealer, as opposed to the 'users' described above. This study has indicated, however, that active involvement is a complex process. Collection and distribution of child pornography is best seen as the more visible portion of a much broader array of activities, both in terms of distribution of child pornography *per se*, and also the broader distribution of information and contacts. In legal terms, there may be something of a grey area here, in that the distribution of information may not always directly relate to an actionable offence, even though it is supportive and central to the development of the process of distributing child pornography. Of course, the two roles may not be mutually exclusive in that a user involved in the distribution of information may very well also be involved in the distribution of child pornography.

Research suggests that the organized structure of this underworld is such that members seem ever-vigilant and primed, not only to deal with any perceived threats posed by 'detractors' but also to avoid detection. This is evidenced by the orchestrating activities of the 'infrastructure advice coordinators', who outline the 'netiquette' of integrating, and navigating safely the virtual paedophile world. The advice given ensures that those with a sexual interest in child sex are acting as a unified cohesive group in the face of potential threats. The advice includes: not responding to 'detractors'; posting inconspicuously; not drawing attention to content of posts; respecting other members of the community; being careful not to do anything to jeopardize their safety.

Presumably, if the current situation of minimal law-enforcement involvement were to change, from the perspective of the user this organizing executive would become more instructive and the process of group cohesiveness that is a hallmark of paedophile activity would become more effective and pose obstacles to law enforcement.

The Internet has many layers, most notably the easily accessible public forums and secondly the private forums that afford a far greater degree of anonymity. The Usenet newsgroups that were researched in this study could be likened to the front end, public forum for the meeting of like-minded people engaged in the discussion of child sex and the posting and trading of child-sex related pictures. But as discussed previously there are many other layers to this distributed communication system, which afford far greater degrees of anonymity and security. These include private email, mailing lists, ICQ, IRC and an ever-evolving set of technologies that are constantly changing and reshaping the Internet at an exponential rate. It seems reasonable to suggest that paedophiles would opt for these more private options for communication if pressure from law enforcement were to become too great in the more public layers.

In most European countries, the possession of child pornography is now an offence. In a sense therefore, the subtlety of an individual's involvement with the process is irrelevant if they possess indecent photographs. The detection of such possession is at one level a technical problem; understanding how addresses work and the use of various tools to log site access are essentially technical issues which can largely be solved given technical expertise and sufficient funding to implement solutions.

Understanding the offence, however, takes us beyond the technical into factors related to the social processes involved, and in particular draws our attention to the offender process. In terms of child protection issues, this is of greater significance than solving the technical issues related to detection of individuals on the Internet. It is at this level that we might begin to understand the relationship between child pornography and sexual assaults on children, and in particular the role that possession of child pornography might play in facilitating and developing the passage from passive 'voyeur' to active 'assaulter'.

If child pornography is a manifestation of fantasy, the question then is one of discovering the relationship between fantasy and offending. Is it reasonable to suggest that there could be an evidential nature to fantasies, given the findings that users are highly selective and highly specific in the pictures they choose to post? This selectivity and specificity is reflected in a study of the fantasies discussed in child-sex-related Internet relay chatrooms.

The Metropolitan Police in London and the Amsterdam Police have experience in analysing child pornographic video material from an evidential perspective. Typically, this seized material used to consist of videos and magazines. The advent of the Internet has introduced a new set of dynamics to the production, distribution and collection of child pornography. The multifaceted layering of communication technologies, confounded by the level of anonymity they afford, poses new challenges to law enforcement and legislative bodies. However, the expertise that has been accumulated in analysing child pornography in the more traditional media could be transplanted to the analysis of child pornography being exchanged via the Internet. This transplanting is a practical and necessary step, and one that has been embarked upon by the COPINE team in cooperation with the Paedophilia Unit of the Metropolitan Police, London, and the Amsterdam Police.

This study has begun to explore the nature of the fantasies involved and shows that a systematic basis to the fantasy quality of child pornography can be described. The two illustrative case-studies outlined in this chapter demonstrate the consistency of highly selective preferences that posters demonstrate in their posting behaviour. From a law-enforcement perspective, what is now needed is an extension of this to relate to actual offending. Can we predict from an analysis of the content of child pornography collections anything about the potential danger of the individuals concerned? Do collections, and the process of collecting, tell us anything about offence liability or provide the basis for risk assessment? We are currently engaged in further exploring these issues. When we look at child pornography on the Internet, we see the visible portion of what is a much larger whole. There are good reasons to suppose that a lot of activity, both related to the distribution of photographs as well as information and contacts, takes place secretly. It is almost impossible to estimate the extent or significance of hidden activity, other than to note its probable scale. Monitoring and controlling is not just a problem related to child pornography; it addresses the same range of issues as other criminal activities related to the Internet. It is unlikely that these will be solved outside of a range of solutions to the broader problems associated with illegal and harmful use of the Internet.

Chapter 13

CHILD PREDATORS ON THE WEB

Debbie Mahoney

Child predators are forming an online community network and virtual bond that is unparalleled in history. The paedophile now has the ability to disguise identity, thus enabling believable presentation as a member of a teen group. This disguise enables the paedophile to target potential victims. Intrusion into the private world of the child and the teenager also provides a quick means of tracking down information on potential victims with very little effort – even when the teen himself has attempted an identity disguise.

Online contact with a potential victim allows the paedophile to slowly build a long-term, online communication prior to attempting to engage the child in off-line, personal and physical contact. Additionally, computer technology and the Internet enables child predators to locate and interact with others more readily than ever before.

Although paedophiles luring children on the Internet is a horrifying problem, the long-term organizational aspects of the predators are more terrifying. The advancement of Internet technology allows paedophiles to exchange information about children in an organized forum. They are able to meet in 'online chat rooms' and educate each other. These online discussions include sharing schemes about how to meet, attract and exploit children, and how to lure the parents of their victims into a false sense of security about the predator's presence within the sanctity of the family structure. It has become an online 'How To' seminar in paedophilia activities.

The range and quality of services offered by the Internet makes its use very attractive for paedophiles. From Illegal and Harmful Use of the Internet, Department of Justice, Equality and Law Reform, Dublin, July 1998.

Instant access to other paedophiles allows for the open discussion of their sexual desires, shared ideas about ways to lure victims, mutual support of their adult-child sex philosophies, and instant access to potential child victims worldwide. Paedophiles are openly uniting against legal authorities and blatantly discussing ways to influence public thinking and deter child exploitation legislation.

It is easy to find and read messages between paedophiles supporting adult-child sex. It is also increasingly common to observe paedophiles in chat rooms, encouraging one another to move forward with advances on new victims and false alliances with the victims' families in what they define as 'loving relationships'.

Paedophile chat rooms, forums, IRC-chat, pagers and newsgroups are filled with information on 'their' boys and girls and 'safety tips' that allow the abuse to remain hidden. Some paedophile websites have information posted telling children that it is okay to be sexual with adults. This is in direct opposition to the messages that advocates, teachers and parents have been trying to instil in our children.

The common gathering place and the resultant support with which child predators are providing each other is probably the paedophile's most significant advantage, and the most troublesome for a concerned public. The computer, a common household fixture, is now a place where paedophiles can go for training and validation by their peer group, through comments such as 'You're okay and what you're doing is okay; don't listen to the rest of the world, just listen to us.'

The larger the sense of community and support that is offered, the bolder paedophiles become in their graphic descriptions of sex with, and exploitation of, children. The added comfort of anonymous email addresses and anonymous surfing is helping paedophiles literally to 'hide in the open'. Child predators appear to be feeling safe enough in their nicknames to openly relate, and brag about, their stories of child exploitation.

While paedophile websites are being tracked down and removed from Internet servers in countries all over the world, paedophiles are still easily finding ways to post websites, webrings, forums and chat rooms. Recent online topics have even focused on fund-raising efforts and plans to purchase a dedicated server for their websites.

The ability to receive and offer comfort within the support of their like-minded group reinforces paedophiles in the belief that their attraction to children and adult-child sex is acceptable. A group of avowed paedophiles has even developed its own creed, 'The Boy Love Manifesto'. It is a prime example of how groups of paedophiles have aligned with each other to share and revel in their mutual sexual appetites for children. Reading the paedophile manifesto, one becomes acutely aware of the dangers of the paedophile world.

While one would like to believe that paedophile websites and child pornography areas are not easy to access, this myth only shows how mistaken we are. With the ability to create and access FTP sites worldwide, the paedophile has the ability to promote criminal behaviour wherever Internet access is available.

Most paedophile pages are not blocked by current software; their ability to promote a positive lifestyle of adult-child sex is not only harmful to children, but makes them more dangerous. Validation of their behaviour can only strengthen their belief that sex with children is natural.

PART TWO

COMBATING CHILD PORNOGRAPHY AND PAEDOPHILIA ON THE INTERNET

WHERE TO DRAW THE LINE?

UNESCO's main concern is the young children of today. It is wasteful, dangerous and immoral to sexually abuse children or to involve them in pornography and acts of paedophilia. This runs diametrically counter to universal social and human values and threatens to destroy the future of society.

While we seek to protect children from the dangers of the Internet, it is equally important to identify and punish the real criminals without destroying the tools. These are the new communication and information technologies, the creative environment that provides the means of transferring culture and education and, unfortunately, child pornography and paedophilia.

Thus, UNESCO has an ethical interest too, namely, in safeguarding freedom of expression. Under the terms of UNESCO's Constitution, the Organization is charged with promoting the free flow of ideas by word and image, and a wider and better-balanced dissemination of information at international, as well as national, levels without any obstacle to the freedom of expression.

On the occasion of the UNESCO meeting on Sexual Abuse of Children, Child Pornography and Paedophilia on the Internet, the Director-General alluded to the need to maintain a broad outlook when he said: '. . . the only way to cure the ills of freedom is to ensure more freedom, and the only way to cure the ills of democracy is to have more democracy'. Censorship of the Internet is not a solution. We should not allow paedophilia, child pornography and child prostitution to erect barriers on the roads of freedom.

Chapter 14

FREEDOM OF SPEECH, INFORMATION AND THE PROTECTION OF PRIVACY

Aidan White

Governments around the world, asserting that they want to protect children, are seeking to eradicate harmful and illegal content on the Internet. As they do so, they must be careful not to undermine fundamental freedoms, in particular the right of citizens to communicate freely, and to enjoy freedom of expression and privacy. New communication systems provide great opportunities to expand the mundane horizons of contemporary society, with greater pluralism and empowerment of citizens who have access to more useful information then ever before. However, this will not happen automatically.

Governments are rightly concerned to ensure that legal protection of social and cultural values continues in the online world, but regulation of the global information structure must not compromise existing rights and liberties. In particular, proposals to censor the Internet – from wherever they originate – must be tested to ensure that they do not violate the right to free expression which is guaranteed in international law. While everyone might agree that illegal online communication – when it is a cover for violent pornography, organized crime, terrorism, racism or hate-mongering – should be subject to law enforcement, arguments continue over how this is to be done.

In October 1998 President Clinton signed into law the Child Online Protection Act which criminalizes the commercial distribution on websites of material that is considered harmful to minors. Freedom of speech groups in the United States have raised protests over the Act, claiming that it may be an infringement of the First Amendment, the United States Constitutional article that forbids Congress from enacting legislation that inhibits freedom of expression. The law also regulates the collection and use of personal information from and about children under the age of 13. This is an important step forward, given the potential for paedophiles and others to invade online privacy.

> Traditional forms of censorship will not operate effectively in the new borderless virtual environment of the Internet and individuals involved with children's use of the Internet, be they parents or educators, must share the responsibility of ensuring that a sage environment is provided. From *Illegal and Harmful Use of the Internet*, Department of Justice, Equality and Law Reform, Dublin, July 1998.

There are, however, doubts as to how effective the law can be in view of the technical problems involved. We all recognize the need for effective safeguards, but at the same time we strive to provide children with the full benefits of interactivity on the worldwide web. The United States law calls for warnings and protective screens ('Are you under 18? If so, click here. . .', etc.) to try to discourage youngsters, but these are minor hurdles for persistent surfers and curious children. Penalties may be high – someone posting a site faces jail and/or a fine of up to US$50,000 for each day that illegal material is exposed on the net – but pinning down offenders is fraught with technical difficulties. The lawmakers themselves recognize the need for other types of action. The Act states that '. . . parents, educators and industry must continue to find ways to protect children from being exposed to harmful material on the Internet'.

The member states of the European Union (EU) have reached broad agreement on the need to make a distinction between illegal content and harmful content. The different categories require different approaches, particularly regarding the use of law to combat offenders. Illegal content will be dealt with by existing law-enforcement agencies according to national law and agreements of judicial cooperation. In order to facilitate the task of the police and public authorities, industry is being encouraged to adopt properly functioning systems of self-regulation (such as codes of conduct and establishment of hot-lines for complaints) which must fit in with national legal norms.

In tackling harmful content the EU gives priority to efforts that enable users to use technical means to filter unsavoury material. The use of content-rating systems, awareness-raising initiatives for parents, and encouraging young people to develop their own self-regulating methods are all part of the EU programme. In May 1998 the European Union Council of Ministers adopted a four-year action plan for promoting safe use of the Internet. This will provide funds for a European network of hot-lines and numerous projects examining filtering, rating and demonstration products designed to reduce the dangers of the Internet, in particular for the protection of minors. However, once again the risks to freedom of expression in such a policy led to some dissent, with criticism voiced in the European Parliament and the Danish Government voting against the action plan.

The fact is, of course, that no amount of action plans and well-intentioned project planning can stop illegal or harmful content on the Internet. Children are often highly skilled in the ways of the computer and the Internet. Many of them learn quickly the art of circumventing 'protective' software, and actions taken at continental level, whether in Europe or the United States, are not enough to address the challenge of a truly global information system. It is clear that world-wide agreements and strategies that involve all the major players – governments, industry, information professionals and civil society groups – are essential to any workable solution.

In 1999 the European Union launched an International Communications Charter which is hoped to set 'a framework for international policy cooperation'. Such cooperation must recognize that in a global context the use of the Internet is already subject to many controls and that the majority of people are still excluded from participation.

While the developed nations wrestle with the dilemma of Internet-content control in contrast to the rights of the child against the need to protect free expression, the rest of the world is struggling to gain access to the Internet itself. On a world-wide level it is estimated that at least 80 per cent of the world's population still lacks the most basic telecommunications which are essential to Internet use. The question of access is an issue closely related to censorship, and it is fundamental to creating the conditions for freedom of information for all. Although opportunities to promote access have never been greater, many governments are imposing limits for a variety of different reasons. In recent years a range of countries, including China, Germany, India, New Zealand, Saudi Arabia, Singapore, the United States and Vietnam, have imposed restrictions on online communications. Some cite economic, political, cultural or public safety as the reason, but the results are the same: a steady erosion of democratic rights.

> The media have undoubtedly contributed to the liberalization of sexually explicit imagery, and to shifts in moral values. Satellite technology, international travel and a breakdown in support infrastructures means that such images are often received in a non-supportive context, or even in a whole society for which they were not specifically intended. The press and media can also contribute greatly to advocacy, underlining positive moral values and human rights. They can support positive family values and inform parents when their children are at risk. They help the children themselves to draw moral lines on their own behaviour and to identify risk factors or situations in which they might be endangered. They are the most powerful educators. Most important of all, press and media have recognised that they are important players in the whole area of commercial sexual exploitation of children, and are actively engaged in debate to examine their role and commit to

the ethical underpinnings of their calling. World Congress Against Commercial Sexual Exploitation of Children: Technology and the Media.

Governments have also recognized that online communication is particularly susceptible to unauthorized snooping. Around the world, police forces and security services are working on joint arrangements to monitor and scrutinize online communication. In most countries the state's right to intercept telephone calls or to open private mail is usually subject to accountable judicial procedures. However, too little is being done to transfer these checks on abuse of power into the virtual environment. There is little regard for the need of citizens to have access to encryption, which can ensure that individuals and groups may communicate without fear of eavesdropping. Lack of information privacy inhibits online speech and limits the diversity of voices on the Internet unnecessarily.

It is in this context of social exclusion, restricted access and unauthorized monitoring that proposals for tougher regulation of online communications must be examined. The risks to our children from abuse of the Internet are self-evident, but with any discussion of risk it is important to realize that the most horrendous possibilities – children being physically abused or abducted – are also the least likely. Statistically, according to the leading children's rights campaigner and journalist Larry Magid, the greatest risk is that a child will encounter people in chat areas and newsgroups who are unpleasant or obnoxious. Only in a very few cases have paedophiles used email, bulletin boards and chat areas to gain a child's confidence and then arrange a face-to-face meeting.

The need to protect children means we should be aware of risks – exposure to inappropriate material, harassment and invasion of privacy – and action needs to be taken to ensure that children are aware that going online is like going outside the home, i.e., there are potential dangers on every street corner. Parents and children together can minimize the risks by setting their own standards and rules for avoiding trouble. Even so, they need help in this process. Industry must adopt, maintain and enforce meaningful codes and standards which can isolate harmful material and help expose the law breakers. Information professionals such as journalists must become aware of the issues involved in protecting the rights of the child. A start in this respect was made by the International Federation of Journalists in 1998, when it adopted an international charter of principles on child rights and the conduct of journalists. However, more needs to be done to provide parents and children with the technical means to create further safeguards against unwarranted intrusion.

For governments, the tendency to intervene and to seek intrusive and inflexible methods of control must be balanced with an urgent need to enshrine freedom of expression and freedom of information as key principles in the development of new information technologies. In particular, restrictions concerning content should be limited to illegal material and direct and immediate incitement of illegal actions; the right to privacy of children and all users needs to be reinforced; and, above all, the crisis of social exclusion which is turning the use of the Internet into a world of haves and have-nots needs to be addressed. A strategy that uses the strength of the Internet to protect its vulnerable users while at the same time investing in greater freedom of information will enhance public confidence and make the virtual world evermore democratic.

Chapter 15

Freedom of information on the Internet: achieving a balance between promotion and protection

Mark Erik Hecht

Several facts are indisputable with regard to encouraging freedom of information in the context of world-wide concern about child pornography and paedophilia on the Internet. Firstly, it is necessary to ensure the greatest dissemination of views on the Internet. On the other hand sexual abuse of children, child pornography and paedophilia, whether directly through personal contact or indirectly via the Internet, is unacceptable in any community. Someone, either an individual, a group of individuals, or an institution, must be responsible for protecting youth from harm or the risk of harm on the Internet. Several basic and fundamental conventions must therefore exist in terms of the content that is suitable to be placed within the reach of children on the Internet. Societies' values need not change simply because technology has advanced.

Given the assumptions noted above, the two critical issues which must be resolved are: *Who* is the most competent to guard these accepted norms and assure their implementation? And to *what* degree is this interference acceptable? This brief examination will not attempt to answer these difficult and controversial queries, rather it will outline the various arguments and evidence that exist in support of, and against, any one particular solution.

The 'Who'

There are several actors who have been – or could be – involved in ensuring freedoms on the Internet, while at the same time being responsible for its content. Each group of individuals offers a unique contribution to achieving this delicate balance.

Users

Common forms of information oversight are: official edicts by governments, Internet service providers (ISPs), and citizen advocacy/public interest coalitions that try to control the extent to which users themselves may access and participate on the Internet. This may require clients to sign agreements as to the content which they will post or to inform an office if they find questionable material while using the service. It is important to note that this is purely voluntary and places the onus on those operating the technology. If users fail to fulfil their obligations, their access may be denied. However, this process is not automatic and there are no legal ramifications likely to follow a breach of these agreements.

> States Parties shall take all appropriate legislative, administrative, social and educational measures to protect the child from all forms of physical or mental violence, injury or abuse, neglect or negligent treatment, maltreatment or exploitation including sexual abuse, while in the care of parent(s), legal guardian(s) or any other person who has the care of the child. Such protective measures should, as appropriate, include effective procedures for the establishment of social programmes to provide necessary support for the child and for those who have the care of the child, as well as for other forms of prevention and for identification, reporting, referral, investigation, treatment and follow-up of instances of child maltreatment described heretofore, and, as appropriate, for judicial involvement. Article 19, United Nations Convention on the Rights of the Child.

Governments

Perhaps the most controversial participants in this discourse are the governments. In all regions of the world, government bodies and agencies have already acted with varying degrees of success to try to regulate the Internet. In its extreme form, some governments have chosen to make the use of the Internet within their jurisdictions illegal. More commonly, governments have tried to find a solution to what is acceptable within its borders, knowing that the technology now operates *sans frontières*. Examples include: the drafting of laws which place obligations on ISPs or users to refrain from acting in an inappropriate manner by placing questionable content on the Internet; the development of license requirements to provide Internet services; the support of undercover operations, through police forces, to monitor and trap offenders within their jurisdictions; and the creation of rating systems to be included on sites based within their countries. It has been suggested however, that since no government can control every potential signal that is beamed into their country or made available through modern telecommunications connections, governments should attempt to impart shared values and establish consensual alliances rather than impose any one set of arbitrary criteria.

Internet service providers

A number of strategies have been utilized by ISPs to assist in monitoring the dissemination of material through their services while at the same time encouraging free dialogue. For example, some ISPs have chosen to censor or filter only the most exploitative material. Other ISPs, however, have implemented hotlines for users to report offensive documents. The ISPs then decide whether the material is indeed questionable and, if so, warn the offender to remove it voluntarily. Finally, certain ISPs have offered their subscribers software packages to block unsuitable information from entering their homes. What must be remembered is that ISPs operate a business. They are distributors that, by their very nature, have neither editorial control nor input. An ISP is contracted to provide bandwidth and disk space irrespective of the content. As such, it is questionable whether ISPs can share any responsibility for material mounted within their fields.

The 'What'

Most of the debate surrounding the standards that should be met for promoting freedom of expression on the Internet in the context of protecting children's rights, appears to result in arguments over analogies. Academics, researchers, activists and social historians have all created, and continue to create, arguments to encourage either greater regulation of the Internet or fewer laws and agreements for these new technologies. When examining the literature, what becomes evident is that the basis for arguing one option over any other is the nature of the medium itself. Three models seem to permeate the discourse:

The Internet is like radio or television

Espoused by individuals who believe that children can truly be protected only when maximum rules govern the Internet, the television or radio comparison seems to be the most intuitive. As with television or radio, there are many channels to choose from, some appropriate for children and some not. In addition, as with television or radio, the Internet can be turned on and off at will; there is dependency on advertising; it may be visual and/or audio; and adults can, and should, ultimately be involved in monitoring its output. As a result, governments, it is argued, must be empowered to create and maintain the same acceptable community standards on the Internet as they do for radio and television. Once such a higher power intervenes, freedom within the medium can be provided within a child-safe framework. The difficulty with this simile is that unlike television or radio, the Internet is interactive. It requires the listener or viewer to make conscious decisions about which sites will be selected, how much time will be spent on each page, what will be done there, and when or if a particular address will be revisited. Unlike television or radio, a person cannot simply turn it on and watch or listen.

The Internet is like the telephone or post office

The telephone or postal service comparison is often cited by individuals who believe that very little interference is necessary, at least from government or non-government organizations, in order to protect children. In this scenario, the Internet is described as enabling private communication between two individuals, or one individual and a much larger group of interested parties. People can freely choose with whom they want to communicate and once their decision is made, only those people can choose to end the relationship. In the same way that parents must teach their children not to talk on the telephone with strangers, or exchange letters with people they have never met, adults must teach the young to do the same on the Internet. Furthermore, as most societies have chosen not to create legal standards for the exchange of dialogue on the telephone or through the mail between consenting parties, societies must refrain from doing so with these newer forms of communication. The difficulty with this thesis is that it describes but one dimension of the medium. The Internet is far more than just a telephone line or mail carrier. It is also the largest telephone and address book in the world, complete with unconfirmed and unsecured information about all its users among its pages.

The Internet is a library

A third oft-quoted analogy is that the Internet is a virtual library. As such, there should be the same freedom of expression and thought that exists in any public library, however, certain mores must also be imposed by its librarians. Few people would argue that publications by authors like Adolf Hitler or Jim Jones do not belong on library shelves, but however, whether they should be catalogued as history and religion is another matter. A uniform agreement among these virtual librarians must be developed, not with a view to removing questionable content, but rather to classifying it appropriately. Only by doing so will a balance be found between encouraging the accessibility of information and its presentation. The problem with this analogy is that although certain materials, such as pornography or hate literature, are clearly unsuitable for a library's holdings, it is much more debatable as to whether they are inappropriate for the Internet.

Conclusion

Balancing the potential good against the potential evils of freedom of information on the Internet, in the context of world-wide concerns about child pornography and paedophilia, requires that balanced safeguards be put in place to ensure that neither the individual interest, nor civic and societal interests are overwhelmed and sacrificed at the expense of the other. Who should decide on this equilibrium and what the safeguards should be requires a more in-depth analysis.

Certain constants do exist, however. No one entity can act individually: promoting and protecting requires all actors to work cooperatively. Governments will have a role to play in achieving this balance, yet whether their function is one of regulation or supervision is debatable. Whatever course of action is taken, limits must be placed on the objectives in the least intrusive manner possible. If not, the restrictions will be ignored by the public. No regulation can be so absolute as to forbid exceptions, such as cases of artistic merit or educational, scientific and medical purposes. The importance of public interest groups and advocacy networks both to monitor abuses of any agreed principles and to educate the actors as to the importance of following directives cannot be underestimated.

NATIONAL AND INTERNATIONAL LAW ENFORCEMENT, LEGAL AND JURIDICAL ASPECTS

The natural reflex in most countries confronted with the problem of child pornography and paedophilia on the Internet is to 'call the police'. But as the following chapters make clear, legislation, legal and law enforcement institutions have been outdistanced by the Internet. If most countries have legislation concerning pornography and child abuse, the global nature of the Internet raises an entirely new panoply of problems of jurisdiction, extraterritoriality and of simply laying hands on a perpetrator, the only trace of whom is a few megabytes on an anonymous hard disk.

Chapter 16

LEGAL ISSUES AND PROBLEMS IN PROTECTING CHILDREN AGAINST PORNOGRAPHY

Ofelia Calcetas-Santos

Constitutional issues

One of the greatest barriers to the installation of aggressive legal response mechanisms for the protection of children from child pornography in cyber-space is the issue of conflict between certain constitutional rights. Among the rights protected in most constitutions that are being cited in arguing against any kind of restriction or regulation of the Internet, are the right to free speech and expression, the right to privacy, and the right for people in general to receive and have access to information and education. Advocates of civil liberties are wary of any interference with the above freedoms and any attempt to restrict them is greeted with cries of censorship. While it is true that some of the objections arise from relevant legal issues and come from very legitimate sources, we also have to recognize the probability that many of those crying 'foul' in the name of civil liberty may have a more nefarious agenda.

> Usually justice follows behind crime, sometimes too far behind. Sir Peter Ustinov, member of the Swiss National Action Group to Protect Innocence in Danger.

On the other hand, activists in the search for a more child-friendly infor-mation highway argue that the rights cited above are not absolute and should be reconciled with other rights when a conflict situation arises. They invoke the same basic constitutional right to privacy, only this time it is in favour of the right of protection of children and not of the purveyors and users of pornography. They accept the right of the public to receive information and educational material but maintain that this must be balanced against the right of children to be protected against any form of sexual exploitation and the broader right of Internet users not to receive unwanted or illegal material.

In discussing constitutionality issues, it is essential to make a distinction between material potentially perceived as harmful or unwanted, such as adult pornography, and material recognized to be illegal *per se,* such as child pornography.

It is difficult to draw the legal line for banning from the Internet material that is freely available in other media, if this material is not illegal but is merely considered undesirable by the general public. The bulk of adult pornographic material is still in print and the right of the public not to be exposed to these materials is recognized to a certain extent by the 'top shelf' policy offered by newsagents. Unfortunately, it is difficult to replicate this 'top shelf' policy on the Internet. There is clearly a need for innovative ways to protect the unsuspecting public from material which, though not illegal, may be perceived as harmful or highly offensive.

The issue of child pornography is quite another matter – it involves material that is *a priori* illegal. Thus, there should be little argument that constitutional rights cannot be invoked to protect the producer or user of child pornography.

Public attitude and lack of awareness

Most parents are chiefly interested in guarding their children from being exposed to pornography, whether depicting adults or children. They probably give little thought to the women and children who are being exploited in the production of this pornography.

Obsolescence of legislation

Developments in cyberspace have essentially rendered existing child pornography legislation obsolete. If it exists at all, most national legislation on child pornography is based on print as the medium, with an actual child as the model. But given today's technological capabilities, which make possible the creation of pseudo-images or 'morphing' of images of children, most legislation prohibiting child pornography has become ineffective. Imagination can run even wilder in computer-generated digital images and animation – the so-called adult cartoons.

Cultural, moral and legal variations in national situations

Pornography on the Internet raises the same problems as any other form of pornography, to the extent that different countries, societies and cultures have different levels of tolerance concerning what constitutes unacceptable material. Cultural and moral standards are quite diverse, and since in most instances these are the determinants of legislation, it is no surprise that the resulting laws are also quite diverse. In most instances subjective standards come into play, which create added problems of implementation and enforcement. An example of this is the obscenity requirement, where the lack of clear guidelines as to what is obscene leaves the determination thereof almost to the sole discretion of the judge who happens to be hearing the case.

Differing national laws on what constitutes pornography; when a young person is no longer classed as a child; which country has jurisdiction; and who is legally responsible for Internet content, mean that securing conviction is no easy task. As one German police officer put it, 'When it comes to hard core pornography, the difficulty for us is that much of what's illegal here in Germany is legal and normal in Scandinavia'.

Lack of trained law-enforcement agents

One very common lament of law-enforcement agents is that the technology available to them is decades behind the sophistication of the equipment being used by child exploiters. This of course leads to a situation where the police are often ill-equipped to understand how to identify not only the producers but the consumers of child pornography.

Lack of adequate response mechanisms

There have been some notable efforts made in some countries and by some international non-governmental organizations to put in place strategies to encourage reporting of infiltrators and users of child pornography on the Internet. The competent authorities in many countries have not yet begun to address this problem. Governments are often discouraged by the persistent myth that the Internet is a vast anarchic network beyond the reach of, and uncontrollable by, government.

Lack of internationally accepted standards

As already discussed above, there is as yet no internationally established and recognized definition of child pornography. It would seem important that standards as to what may be considered child pornography should be adopted, also extending to pseudo-images or morphed images of children. The argument that there are no victims if actual children are not used in the production of the pornography has no validity. In child pornography, there are two reprehensible acts. One is committed against the specific children used in its production, and the other is against all children in general who are threatened and treated as sex objects by child pornography.

The United States' Child Pornography Prevention Act of 1996 enlarged the federal definition of child pornography, which previously covered only erotic pictures of actual minors. Section 2 of the 1996 Act explains why pseudo-photographs of children should also be illegal:

> Computer-generated child pornography results in many of the same types of harm, and poses the same danger to the well-being of children, as photographic child pornography, and provides a compelling governmental interest for prohibiting the production, distribution, possessing, sale or viewing of all forms of child pornography, including computer-generated depictions which are, or appear to be, of children engaging in sexually explicit conduct.

> States Parties shall take measures to combat the illicit transfer and non-return of children abroad. To this end, States Parties shall promote the conclusion of bilateral or multilateral agreements or accession to existing agreements. Article 11, United Nations Convention on the Rights of the Child.

Some significant international developments in the search for solutions

In the United States, one solution that is being promoted is software programs that will screen out sexually explicit material. President Clinton has stated that he supports a rating system on the Internet, where material would be rated so that software programs could screen out child pornography. Not everyone welcomes that prospect, however. There is vocal opposition to the development of rating systems, most forcibly expressed by the American Civil Liberties Union (ACLU) which does not see enhanced consumer choice but the danger that authoritarian interests could lock out unpopular views. They fear that minority opinions or tastes will be excluded.

Disney and Time Warner have announced that they are establishing 'whitelisting services', that is, Internet subscription services that give access not to the whole of the Net, but only to the parts they have vetted. This would enable different groups to use their own standards for vetting materials on the Internet.

The United Kingdom ISP Demon Internet is developing and testing a system that automatically weeds out child pornography and other illegal material from Usenet newsgroups. The engine scans the 26,000 newsgroups, looking for material which has already been reported to the Internet Watch Foundation (IWF) and then removes it so that the same may not be reposted. IWF is an independent organization dealing with the problem of illegal material on the Internet.

Singapore is regulating the content of the Internet through a Class Licence Scheme, where ISPs and Internet content providers (ICPs) are required to block out objectionable sites as directed by the Singapore Broadcasting Authority.

In India, the government has attempted to prevent misuse of the Internet by limiting access to the academic world, and not making it available to the individual or commercial user.

In Sweden, a Bill on Responsibility for Electronic Notice Boards was introduced. Under the Bill a provider would be obliged to give users of the service information about his or her identity and to what extent incoming messages become available to other users. Providers would be obliged to remove, or otherwise prevent continued dissemination, certain categories of message from their services, e.g., incitement to criminal acts, vilification of groups of people, child pornography or the unlawful depiction of violence. The providers of electronic notice boards would not generally be obliged to screen all incoming messages, but if a provider is informed that it is assisting dissemination of these categories of criminal speech it would have to act to prevent further dissemination. This, however, raises the question of how an ISP can determine whether material is legal or not, even if the ISP is aware of it being broadcast. Furthermore, it is impossible for a large server to scrutinize all transmissions.

In the Netherlands, the 'Hotline for Child Pornography on Internet' operates by asking Internet users to report any child pornography that they find. Once a site is reported, the website provider will ask the issuer of the material (if traceable) to remove it from the Internet, and will report that person to the police if he or she fails to do so. The hotline is conceived as an initiative against censorship by indirectly targeting the poster of illegal child pornography instead of whole areas of information and communication.

In Denmark, the National Commissioner of Police has established a home page on the Internet where people can report information on suspected distribution of child pornography through the Internet directly to the police.

In Australia, the Australian Broadcasting Authority, a statutory body, has produced a report supporting a code of conduct established by private industry, subject to registration with a public authority.

Chapter 17

LEGAL AND JURIDICAL ASPECTS:
EXTRATERRITORIAL LAW AND EXTRADITION

Pierre Dionne

The United Nations Convention on the Rights of the Child is the main impetus behind efforts to curb the international dimension of child sexual exploitation, including child pornography and paedophilia on the Internet. The United Nations General Assembly adopted this Convention on 20 November 1989 and it came into force on 2 September 1990, after having been ratified by the twenty States required under Article 49. This convention is unique among international human rights instruments in that it covers the full range of human rights, not only civil and political but also economic, social and cultural. Besides this wide scope it also contains two major conceptual innovations. The first is that the principle of the 'best interests of the child' should be the guiding principle in 'all actions concerning children' (Article 3 [1]). The second is that the views of children should be 'given due weight in accordance with the age and maturity of the child' (Article 12 [1]).

The Convention on the Rights of the Child does not stand alone. It is an integral part of a human rights agenda with a long history, which has gained increasing impetus since 1945 in the context of the United Nations. As the Preamble to the Convention makes clear, it is fundamentally based in the body of previous United Nations human rights instruments, and has its own history within the human rights project. The first five-point declaration of children's rights, known as the Declaration of Geneva, was adopted by the Fifth Assembly of the League of Nations in 1924, and the United Nations Convention on the Rights of the Child should be viewed as the culmination of more than six decades of activity within the international community on behalf of children.

It is important to note that in recent years a change of emphasis has taken place in the field of international human rights. The initial focus was on setting standards, as well as identifying and denouncing violations of rights. Now there is an increasing interest in ensuring the effective implementation of human rights instruments, together with the progressive achievement of the provisions they contain. This is especially true with respect to the United Nations Convention on the Rights of the Child. Although there is considerable interest in the more formal matters, such as the relevant changes in the domestic legislation of States Parties and States Party reports to the Committee on the Rights of the Child (for which provision is made in Articles 43 and 44), there is also considerable pressure from intergovernmental agencies and interested sectors of civil society to ensure that administrative and operational procedures are put in place in order to ensure effective implementation and monitoring.

The Sexual exploitation of children

One of the motives for establishing a specific United Nations Convention on the Rights of the Child is the recognition of their special vulnerability. Thus, the Convention contains a number of articles concerned with protecting them against abuse and exploitation. Among these Article 34, which deals with the sexual exploitation of children, is acknowledged to be one of the most important:

> States Parties undertake to protect the child from all forms of sexual exploitation and sexual abuse. For these purposes, States Parties shall in particular take all appropriate national, bilateral and multilateral measures to prevent:
> (a)   The inducement or coercion of a child to engage in any unlawful sexual activity;
> (b)   The exploitative use of children in prostitution or other unlawful sexual practices;
> (c)   The exploitative use of children in pornographic performances and materials.

The current prominence given by the international community to this article is based on a recognition of the scale of harm involved. This refers not only to the traumatic effects on individual children, but also to the number of children reported to be affected. Within the provisions of the Convention, the theme of the sexual exploitation of children also includes those articles that call for the provision of the services and resources for children that should prevent sexual exploitation taking place, as well as articles that require protection against other forms of exploitation (Articles 32-6), and against the sale and traffic of children. It is also important to take into account articles intended to provide support for parents (Articles 19, 26 and 27) so that the sexual exploitation of children does not become an income-generating mechanism within family survival strategies. In addition, the principles of self-determination and expression, enshrined in Article 12, but also dealt with in other 'participation' articles (Articles 13-16), are important for discussions of children's consent to sexual activity.

> Because of the essential nature of the Internet, there are serious limits to what any one country can achieve on its own in the area of addressing the downside issues. The Internet itself is an international phenomenon in every sense of the word and any effective response will hinge on high levels of international cooperation. From *Illegal and Harmful Use of the Internet*, Department of Justice, Equality and Law Reform, Dublin, July 1998.

The responses of the international community

A crucial catalyst for the development of international awareness of the dimensions of the sexual exploitation of children was the World Congress against the Commercial Sexual Exploitation of Children, held in Stockholm, Sweden, in August 1996. Although the impetus for this event came initially from the non-governmental sector (NGOs), the impressive involvement of governments and intergovernmental organizations resulted in a number of significant advances. These include: a focus on the international dimension of the sexual exploitation of children; increased awareness of the sexual exploitation of children; an understanding of the need for implementing the provisions of relevant human rights instruments; and networking among governments and NGOs, which represents a hitherto unrealized alliance between States and civil society, as well as opportunities for mutual learning.

Thus, it is now understood that there is a need for systems to be put in place to combat the sexual exploitation of children at national and international levels. Both governments and civil society realize that the challenge no longer consists simply in promoting a campaign of awareness-raising. The priority is implementation in terms of legislative changes, not only of the United Nations Convention on the Rights of the Child and related instruments, but also the protection of children and the prosecution of offenders. One response to the Congress and its Draft Declaration and Agenda for Action has been that several governments have adopted, and others are considering, new legislation designed to combat the international aspects of the sexual exploitation of children.

One further important element in the background to the Public Hearings is a continuing debate about the development of an optional protocol to the United Nations Convention on the Rights of the Child, dealing specifically with sexual exploitation. This protocol specifically addresses the international dimensions of sexual exploitation, particularly the activities that are often described as 'sex tourism'. According to Margaret A. Healey, under the Draft Optional Protocol, parties would assume a substantial obligation to cooperate with other states to further the prevention, detection, prosecution and punishment for crimes of sexual exploitation of, or trafficking in, children. The burden on parties would be greater than that imposed by the United Nations Convention on the Rights of the Child which generally obliges States Parties to take national, bilateral and multilateral action to prevent child prostitution and exploitation, but does not require extraterritorial legislation or any other specific measure. In addition, Article 1 of the Draft Optional Protocol asserts that the sexual exploitation of, and trafficking in, children constitute 'crimes against humanity', placing them in the same category as war crimes such as wilful killing, torture, genocide and unlawful mass deportations.[1]

Extraterritorial legislation has, therefore, been identified as one potentially powerful tool in the implementation of those provisions of international human rights instruments that are directed towards protecting children against sexual exploitation.

Extraterritorial legislation

There are clearly several options for action that can be taken at the national and international levels to combat the sexual exploitation of children, one of which is the adoption of legal measures. As bilateral extradition treaties are often limited in scope, a number of countries have indeed enacted extraterritorial legislation, making it possible for them to prosecute sex tourists or others who have committed a sexual offence against a child while abroad, including child pornography. In addition, intergovernmental action has resulted in the drafting of the Optional Protocol mentioned above, which, if adopted, could oblige a State Party to adopt or adapt extraterritorial laws to enable the prosecution of offenders for sexual crimes committed against children abroad.

Extraterritorial legislation is neither limited to the sexual exploitation of children nor is it new. Over twenty countries allow it to be applied in the case of sex offenders. This has been achieved through different approaches. Some states have a provision within their laws which extends their jurisdiction to acts committed by their nationals while abroad. Others have amended their criminal or penal laws to include the specific crime of child

1. Healey, Margaret A., 1995, 'Prosecuting child sex tourists at home: do laws in Sweden, Australia and the United States safeguard the rights of children as mandated by international law?' In *Fordham International Law Journal*, Vol. 18, 1852–1923, p. 1879.

sexual exploitation through 'sex tourism' or 'child prostitution'. Finally, some have simply adopted new laws in order to deal with the eventuality of one of their nationals sexually exploiting a child while outside the country's normal territorial jurisdiction. Thus far, however, even in cases that do not involve the sexual exploitation of children, the number of prosecutions based on principles of extraterritorial jurisdiction is very small. Experience in this field is therrefore limited and the international community might be said to be still in a learning phase.

> A male university professor who smuggled a poor 15-year-old boy from Honduras into Florida and had sexual relations with him for almost a year became the first person convicted under a new U.S. law barring 'sex tourism' targeting minors. Reuters, International Herald Tribune, 4 March 1999.

There are a number of principles that govern the conditions under which a government can extend its jurisdiction to criminal acts committed beyond the boundaries of its own territory. In brief, these are: what is called the 'active personality' of the offender, which means that jurisdiction can be extended outside national territory to acts committed by nationals; the 'passive personality' of the victim, whose nationality provides the basis for the establishment of extraterritorial jurisdiction; the principle of protection, through which states reserve the right to take action with respect to acts that threaten their national security; and the principle of universality, which refers to 'universal crimes', sometimes called 'crimes against humanity'.

One factor complicating the understanding and application of extraterritorial legislation is that these principles are neither universally agreed upon nor universally applied.

Other legal concepts that are important in this field are: double criminality, which entails that, for extraterritorial legislation to be used, the act involved must be illegal according to the laws of the countries of the offender and of the country where the crime was committed; and double jeopardy (*non bis in idem*), whereby a person who has been acquitted or convicted of an offence cannot be prosecuted again for that same offence.

In the case of child sexual exploitation, associated notably with sex tourism, the responsibility of corporate bodies, such as tour companies, becomes important. Where this exists, it not only allows companies involved in the sex industry to be found criminally liable, but also subject to seizure and forfeiture of assets and responsible for damages to exploited children. A further important principle in the sexual exploitation of children is the legal age of consent to sexual acts. This may establish the grounds for prosecution, but may also be a complicating factor if the age of consent in the offender's country differs from that of the country where the offence was committed. Finally, various legal principles governing the period of time that can elapse between offence and prosecution are of practical importance, given the time-consuming nature of negotiations between states with different legislative and administrative mechanisms.

Extraterritorial legislation is not new, but has gained a new dimension within the context of international concern about the commercial sexual exploitation of children, particularly 'sex tourism'. The 1996 Stockholm Congress against the Commercial Sexual Exploitation of Children produced a Declaration and a Plan of Action which calls *inter alia* for the enactment of extraterritorial legislation, and was adopted by the Congress, including the 119 states that sent representatives. Thus, in the case of sex tourism, it calls for action from all states to:

> [...] develop or strengthen and implement laws to criminalise the nationals of the countries of origin when committed against children in the countries of destination ('extraterritorial criminal laws'); promote extradition and other arrangements to ensure that a person who exploits a child for sexual purposes in another country (the destination country) is prosecuted either in the country of origin or the destination country; strengthen laws and law enforcement, including confiscation and seizure of assets and profits, and other sanctions, against those who commit sexual crimes against children in destination countries; and share relevant data.

> Cybercrime challenges the traditional notions of national or state laws because it is borderless, has no frontiers. Today we need transnational *tools* and international co-operation. Former Director-General of UNESCO

While in some cases, adopting and implementing extraterritorial legislation is seen as having a deterrent effect, extraterritorial legislation is only one tool among many in the fight to protect children from sexual exploitation, and should not be regarded as an end in itself. As noted by some, the primary responsibility for protecting children against the international dimensions of the sexual exploitation of children rests with the country in which the offence takes place. Others argue that the roots of the problem, especially in developing countries, cannot be eradicated because they arise from poverty. A swift and forceful implementation of legal changes must therefore be accompanied by social action aimed at eliminating the need for children to generate income in the market for sex tourism and other forms of exploitation.

Implementation of extraterritorial legislation, in the few cases that have so far been pursued, has depended largely on personal contacts between professionals in the countries involved, and the commitment and often ingenuity of individuals as well as voluntary action. The costs involved in bringing cases to court are high, partly because of the need for law enforcement agencies and witnesses to travel between countries, but also because of factors such as translation and interpretation. Up to now, voluntary and individual action have reduced costs to a certain extent and made it possible to demonstrate that extraterritorial legislation can be used effectively to combat the international dimension of the sexual exploitation of children. However, it is apparent that in the long term the success of extraterritorial legislation should depend not on occasional volunteer activities, but rather on being able to establish sustainable systems, based on what has been learned through the cases pursued thus far, and on finding sufficient resources to support such systems.

Efforts to combat direct forms of sexual exploitation of children, such as in prostitution, must now be accompanied by efforts to curb more indirect forms of sexual exploitation of children like child pornography, with particular reference to dissemination of pornographic material on electronic networks such as the Internet. Governments, it seems, are considering ways in which extraterritorial legislation might be used to combat the international distribution of pornographic material relating to children. Application of extraterritorial legislation in this respect may be less concerned with the production of pornographic materials than with their distribution. Thus, wide-ranging provisions within New Zealand legislation refer to acquiring, transporting and publishing child pornography by any means, 'whether by written, electronic or any other form of communication and including the distribution of information'. The government of France includes within its definition of pornography virtual images as well as non-pornographic images designed to be used by paedophiles, thus acknowledging the importance of the ulterior use to which images are put, as much as the actual exploitation of individual children in the production of pornography.

To conclude, the International Tribunal for Children's Rights adopted a set of recommendations following the First Hearings held in Paris in October 1997. Although these recommendations are targeted specifically at the adoption and implementation of extraterritorial legislation, they contain some very important elements relevant to all initiatives undertaken in the struggle against the international dimensions of child sexual exploitation.

Recommendations of the International Tribunal for Children's Rights on the use of extraterritorial legislation to combat sexual exploitation of children

THE MEMBERS OF THE INTERNATIONAL TRIBUNAL FOR CHILDREN'S RIGHTS,

Considering that, in adopting the UN Convention on the Rights of the Child, the international community has reiterated its interest and determination in promoting the well-being of children and the respect of their rights;

Recalling that, pursuant to articles 19, 32 to 36 of the UN Convention on the Rights of the Child, States Parties have undertaken to protect children from all forms of abuse and exploitation, including all forms of sexual exploitation and sexual abuse;

Recalling that, to this end, States Parties to the UN Convention on the Rights of the Child have undertaken to take all appropriate national, bilateral and multilateral measures to prevent: 1) the inducement or coercion of a child to engage in any unlawful sexual activity, 2) the exploitative use of children in prostitution or other unlawful sexual practices, and 3) the exploitative use of children in pornographic performances and materials;

Propose the following recommendations:

The protection of children must be the first priority in all legislation and implementation of legislation aiming to combat the international dimensions of the sexual exploitation of children. Without prejudice to the presumption of innocence of the accused, this means that no harm should be caused to children in the course of investigations carried out for, or legal processes involved in, prosecuting and convicting those who commit sexual offences against children.

This principle entails that:

a) investigations should not be carried out in ways that:
   (i) are psychologically damaging to children;
   (ii) put children at risk of intimidation or physical danger;

b) children must be protected from intimidation and physical danger, as well as undue disruption to their lives, identities or economic security, during the period before and during court proceedings;

c) the best interests of the child (Article 3.1 of the Convention on the Rights of the Child) and the right to have his/her opinion taken into account in all decisions taken on her/his behalf (Article 12 of the Convention on the Rights of the Child) should be the guiding principles in decisions about whether a child should:
   (i)   travel to the country of the accused to give evidence;
   (ii) give evidence by video link, either between countries or in the country of the accused;
   (iii) give evidence in court;
   (iv) give evidence in some other place;
   In all such decisions due consideration should be given to the child's age, maturity and culture.

d) child victims in sexual exploitation cases pursued through the application of extraterritorial legislation should not be cross-examined aggressively and in particular not to a greater extent than adults or than children who are nationals of the country of the accused. Domestic legislation should be amended to ensure that this is the case;

e) a child's prior reputation should be inadmissible evidence;

f) the interpretation of rules and procedures should be flexible in order to reflect the principle of the protection of children. Systems should adjust to the special vulnerabilities of children;

g) interpreters in investigative and legal proceedings should receive specialist training to enable them to deal sensitively with sexually exploited children. They should be able to express themselves fluently in both the dialect of the child and the language of the court. They should be aware of the cultural mores of the child's society and social group;

h) law enforcement and legal professionals should receive specialist training in communicating with and listening to sexually exploited children;

i) victim support services should be alerted to and involved in all cases involving extraterritorial legislation and the sexual exploitation of children to provide culturally-appropriate counselling and socio-economic support to children at all stages in the process, including follow-up;

j) children who have been victims of sexual exploitation or traffic should not be repatriated unless follow-up support can be provided and certainly not if there is evidence that repatriation might threaten their physical security;

k) the implementation and consequences of statutes of limitation should be researched and reviewed.

The implementation of extraterritorial legislation with respect to the sexual exploitation of children should have the objective of establishing sustainable systems for prosecuting individual and corporate offenders. Such systems should:

a) not rely on voluntary or individual efforts;

b) be able to deal with cases systematically, rather than on an occasional basis;

c) be cost effective;

d) be seen to be effective so that they act as a deterrent;

To this end, international co-operation should be encouraged and reinforced through agreements at international, regional and bilateral levels, building on the experiences gained from the implementation of existing memoranda of understanding, such as those between the governments of the United Kingdom and the Philippines, and Germany and Thailand.

These agreements should entail:

a) co-operation between relevant ministries;

b) co-operation between law enforcement agencies;

c) co-operation between legal professionals;

d) exchange of information and the development of data bases;

e) training at all levels, including specialist interpreters;

f) support and resources;

g) exchange of research results;

h) monitoring and documentation of the implementation of extraterritorial legislation and bilateral agreements.

International co-operation should include, but not be limited to, further discussion of the Draft Optional Protocol to the United Nations Convention on the Rights of the Child on the Sale of Children, Child Prostitution and Child Pornography.

A working group should be established at international level to develop a separate treaty that would reconcile the legal, administrative and investigative rules of concerned nations in order to facilitate the implementation of extraterritorial legislation in cases of the sexual exploitation of children. The agenda of this working group should include, but not be limited to:

a) definitions of sexual offences against children;

b) reconciliation of chronological ages of children with respect to sexual offences against children and the age of consent to sexual activities;

c) the inter-relationship between rules of double criminality and the definition of ages;

d) international agreements about, and the possible elimination of, double criminality;

e) rules concerning testimony;

f) standards of acceptable proof.

To ensure effective co-operation at international level between States and civil society, resources should be sought for the establishment of a specialised, permanent forum for the exchange of information, including a web site on the Internet.

Training of relevant professionals, including law enforcement personnel, judges, magistrates, welfare workers and researchers, should take into account the special requirements of child victims and child witnesses, with respect to the provisions of the United Nations Convention on the Rights of the Child. In addition, specialist training for national level focal points within all professions that are involved in the implementation of extraterritorial legislation in combating the international dimensions of the sexual exploitation of children should take place, with particular reference to the experience gained in existing training programmes. Training issues include, but are not limited to:

a) communicating with and listening to children;

b) cultural meanings and linguistic issues involved in understanding the sexual exploitation of children;

c) the development of 'child-friendly' investigative and legal procedures;

d) appropriate research skills.

Research and documentation should provide the basis for informed collaboration. In particular, research is required on:

a) monitoring and evaluation of the implementation of extraterritorial legislation in combating the international dimensions of the sexual exploitation of children;

b) the impact of training programmes for professionals in this field;

c) the potential of extraterritorial legislation in combating the dissemination of child pornography, particularly through electronic networks such as the Internet;

d) the impact on children of involvement in international legal action against child sex offenders.

Chapter 18

INTERNATIONAL COOPERATION IN LAW ENFORCEMENT

Agnès Fournier de Saint Maur

How can one define child pornography in the context of international law enforcement cooperation to combat paedophilia and child pornography on the Internet? Interpol, the International Criminal Police Organization, has a standing working group on offences against minors working on these matters, and their work is based on the following definition:

> Child pornography is the consequence of the exploitation or sexual abuse perpetrated against a child. It can be defined as any means of depicting or promoting sexual abuse of a child, including print and/or audio, centred on sex acts or the genital organs of children.

To illustrate in concrete terms the discussion which follows, one can cite a few figures. On 2 September 1998, 96 people were arrested in twelve countries. The biggest equipment seizure involved a Finn at whose home 48 gigabytes of child pornography files were seized. In the United Kingdom, the size of the seizure was estimated at around a minimum of 250,000 images. In the United States, the biggest seizure at an individual's home was 75,000 images, total seizures amounted to 500,000 images and more than 120 videos of child pornography. Once collected, the aggregate total of seizures for all of the countries therefore runs to huge amounts which, even if one considers that images have been duplicated many times over, give an insight into the suffering of the children involved in the production of this material and the role played by the Internet in the transmission and exchange of child pornography.

In their little worlds in which children have their existence, there is nothing so finely perceived and so finely felt, as injustice. . . . Charles Dickens, *Great Expectations.*

As this case demonstrates, computer technology has transformed the production of child pornography into a sophisticated, universal and cottage industry. Anyone with access to a computer and a modem can connect to online commercial services and the Internet, this remarkable network linking some 100 million people to each other in the four corners of the world. In this way, the Internet is fast becoming the most significant factor in the sexual abuse of children and the principal means of exchange of child pornography. It defies any simple comparison with existing media or with the other traditional modes of communication.

Among the techniques available to paedophiles for exchanging and/or selling their material, one can cite high volume and high-speed image transmission capture, data encryption, and anonymous remailing through specialized companies. Today, fixed or moving images are increasingly mobile, recorded productions are increasingly presented as live productions, meaning that children are raped and tortured 'to order', with simultaneous transmission to the computers of interested parties, images are modified to create new ones, and so on. The boundaries of horror will continue to be pushed back with the assistance, albeit unintentional, of technological progress.

The World Congress against Commercial Sexual Exploitation of Children, held in Stockholm in 1996, drew attention to the problem of the circulation of child pornography on communication networks and strongly argued that the time had come to criminalize the simple possession of such content. In most cases, production, distribution, importation and advertising of child pornography are proscribed by states but, unfortunately, rarely its mere possession. It is, therefore, important at the outset to define a set of common standards on what should be considered illegal. Some will say, however, that whatever we may do the law is impotent, given the extreme flexibility of the network which will make any identification and, by extension, assertion of recognizable responsibility, impossible. This argument is advanced by the mass media and by many legal experts, but not by technicians who believe that the possibilities for control go much further that what is claimed.

As an international police organization, Interpol has a duty to ensure that criminals cannot act with impunity and are prevented from exploiting technological advances to their own ends, believing themselves immune from prosecution. What are the problems, from the legal and law enforcement standpoints, that we face today? What solutions or, more modestly, beginnings of responses can we offer? These two questions are fundamental.

Legal aspects

Although computers can be used to carry out quite remarkable and valuable tasks, their proliferation and the advent of online communication pose considerable challenges in all legislative areas. According to international criminal law, the state that has jurisdiction is the one on whose territory the offence was committed. The real problem with the Internet is, therefore, determining the country of the crime, which is complicated by the international scope of the network.

> Tracing and proving illegal use of the Internet presents unique law enforcement challenges. Despite a proliferation of addressing systems, anonymous use of the Internet is still relatively easy and identifying the source of material placed on the Internet can be extremely difficult and indeed, sometimes impossible. The ease with which child pornography can be copied and disseminated in digital form is a serious barrier to any enforcement strategy which seems to contain the problem. From *Illegal and Harmful Use of the Internet,* Department of Justice, Equality and Law Reform, Dublin, July 1998.

Indeed, in a universal context in which illicit information crosses several legal administrations in different states, at the speed of light, what criteria should be used to identify the locality of the offence? Can rules which apply to only a single territory and, therefore, only partly address the question of the facts, be deemed effective? Furthermore, the question of competence in respect of child pornography is even more complex, as the rules applied in each society are entirely subjective. The terms 'child' and 'child pornography' have different legal definitions the world over and sometimes even under different jurisdictions within the same state.

In international criminal law, three theories overlap and intertwine with regard to the problem of determining the country of the crime committed via the Internet: the theory of *Action* according to which the offence is situated in the very place it was committed in the strictest sense of the word; the theory of *Result* which, in turn, is based on the determination of the place where damage has been suffered; and lastly, the theory of *Ubiquity,* an amalgamation of the two preceding considerations, which makes law enforcement possible wherever criminal data are accessible, from issue to reception.

According to this theory, we could, therefore, be faced with a plethora of laws that could be applied, as there will be as many laws as the number of states traversed via the network, if only for a fraction of a second. This multiplicity of legislation and of theories might seem to enhance the idea of creating a legal instrument with supranational scope, vested with the authority to regulate everything. However, given the wide diversity of states, no single regulatory body could feasibly win the confidence of them all. The best solution, and the one advocated by Interpol, would be to work on the basis of the criminal law of each state and strive to achieve a degree of legal harmonization first at the regional, and then at the international level. We have effectively noted that, despite the inherently international, context of the Internet network, it is first and foremost at the national level that authority and competence are centred.

One final legal aspect concerns the way in which offences are handled by the many and varied legal systems. Although France and the United States, for instance, agree that child pornography and sexual abuse of minors constitute serious offences, the two countries have a very different approach in keeping with their respective legal traditions. Indeed, in the United States, the First Amendment of the Constitution, guaranteeing freedom of expression, can lead to certain excesses which, unfortunately in some instances, benefit the criminals.

Hence our role is to determine what is technically possible and economically reasonable, and to strike a balance between the protection of freedom of expression and the right to a private life on the one hand, and, on the other hand, the protection of the dignity and rights of children, mindful that, according to the terms of the United Nations Convention on the Rights of the Child, the superior interest of the child must take precedence over all other considerations.

Law enforcement aspects

The responsibility of law enforcement agencies is to identify offenders and then demonstrate their alleged responsibility. It often proves difficult, however, to search for the respective responsibilities in the chain of communication, from the input of content to its access by the end user, owing to a lack of available resources and specialist technical personnel.

For a long time now, the Interpol working group dedicated to these issues has been stressing the need for specially trained police officers, but this drives home the root of the problem, namely, that specialists in crimes against children are not always specialists in computing. They quite often do not have the necessary equipment to track offenders on the Internet. There is, therefore, a disproportionate knowledge gap between criminals and police services when it comes to using the Internet. Happily, this situation is about to change, thanks to the pressure of events and to the commitment of the law enforcement officers themselves to doing their work. Thus, increasingly, national units are being set up specifically to combat criminal use of the Internet. Lastly, despite the existence of national laws banning the acts in question, too many culprits are still situated outside the scope of their application through the interplay of borders and the limitation of the territorial competence of members of the police force.

Consequently, Interpol recognizes the fundamental role of police cooperation and its own role in the definition of strategies for action at the international level. Interpol's primary mission is to facilitate and strengthen international police cooperation so as to increase the effectiveness of the fight against international crime and also against the illegal use of new technologies. In keeping with this, we believe that priority must be given to the adequate training of law enforcement officers in order to heighten their specialist skills as well supplying them with high-performance computer equipment.

In parallel, more proactive than reactive police intervention techniques, such as infiltration techniques used to identify and track criminals, will offer additional guarantees of efficiency. These investigation techniques must be widely utilized so that current disparities existing at this level do not hinder the success of police operations. The Internet must be the object of careful and reasonable police surveillance so as to protect our children without encroaching on the freedom of communication and information. Because of its mission, Interpol must play a catalytic and centralizing role in this field.

Lastly, we would sincerely like to see the Internet remain a communication and information exchange system accessible to all, but free from criminal use. Private enterprises must take a determined stance alongside law enforcement agencies to put an end to the activities of criminals and thus work together towards a common goal.

> What will it mean to live in the borderless world of cyberspace? We are well aware that the anarchic Internet is no respecter of borders and this leads to an inevitable conflict with most of our current laws which are based on a border mentality. While there are obvious similarities between most laws in most countries, the legal systems which govern behaviour only apply until you cross the border. Legal systems were formed to protect one particular nation state and are still largely based on national cultural values which are effective only within the borders of that country. When we can cross borders as easily as we cross the street, it offers unbelievable possibilities for criminals and many ordinary people who see a chance to beat the system. Ron O'Grady, Chairman of ECPAT, Opening Address at the Child Pornography on the Internet Experts Meeting, Lyon.

It is essential that the computer industry quickly comes to the realization that it has a responsibility and a role to play in the conservation of evidence of traffic in child pornography, on the Internet as well as in the transmission of these data to the competent law enforcement services. In this way, these companies could make an effective contribution to the prevention of sexual abuse of children. Computer industry leaders are unfortunately not yet, and not all, convinced that this responsibility is incumbent on them and still too often refuse to support police efforts on various and sundry pretexts.

Conclusion

Finally, there is the need to educate the public. It has to be provided with clear explanations concerning the advantages and dangers of the Internet so that it too can adopt a responsible attitude. Professionals of the law and its application have a duty to sensitize net users and to mobilize society as a whole. Interpol stands ready to work jointly with the designated persons to establish an international code of conduct and ethics banning criminal use of the fantastic means of communication that is the Internet.

In 1997, Interpol signed an agreement with the Universal Postal Union recognizing the importance of trafficking in child pornography through the postal services and the need for close cooperation between the two international organizations. It is Interpol's wish and hope that, in the near future, a representative body of the private enterprises managing the Internet will be created heralding the possibility of concluding a similar partnership on trafficking in child pornography by computer.

One should not philosophize on the subject of recording sexual abuse of children nor consider this only as a source of entertainment or expression of sexual fantasy. It is a shameful abuse of power. It is for this reason that we, the civil society, the private sector and governmental authorities must commit ourselves to a merciless war on criminals who abuse children. The dissemination and commercialization of the visual representation of sexual abuse committed against the person of a child is a phenomenon than can and must cease, if we use our joint action to assure our children's future. It is intolerable that they should be treated and used as mere sexual objects, consumer goods to satisfy the criminal sexual impulses of some people, as tradable goods for profit. It is all the more intolerable that modern societies accept this deadly trade though their silence and passive complicity.

Interpol has accordingly committed itself to this struggle and risen to the challenge, to ensure that nowhere in the world is safe for criminals and other exploiters of children.

Chapter 19

CASA ALIANZA'S LEGAL WORK IN CENTRAL AMERICA

Bruce Harris

Casa Alianza has been working in Central America since 1981, serving an estimated 100,000 street children in Mexico and Central America. More than 4,500 street boys and girls, between the ages of four or five and eighteen, receive both residential and non-residential services from the agency each year: long-term rehabilitation of street boys and girls; family reintegration; drug rehabilitation; a programme for adolescent mothers and their babies; and life and job skills training. More than anything, however, there is a loving, supportive environment in which severely emotionally damaged street children are given back their childhood. Casa Alianza is a place for second chances.

Since the early 1990s, Casa Alianza has opened legal aid offices in each of our sites. The goal of these legal services is to protect the children's most basic human rights: the right to live; not to be beaten or tortured, especially by the authorities, and the right to be protected from sexual abuse, among many others.

To date, Casa Alianza has almost 600 criminal proceedings active in local courts in Costa Rica, Guatemala, Honduras, Mexico and Nicaragua. There are another ten cases before the Inter-American Commission on Human Rights (part of the Organization of American States) and one before the Inter-American Court on Human Rights in Costa Rica. The latter is the first ever case heard by this prestigious court involving child victims of human rights abuses. Casa Alianza and the Center for Justice and International law (CEJIL) are suing the State of Guatemala for the torture and murder of five street children in Guatemala in 1990.

The Internet operates on an international basis. The law operates on a territorial basis. Thus we have the genesis of many of the legal issues surrounding the Internet. From *Illegal and Harmful Use of the Internet*, Department of Justice, Equality and Law Reform, Dublin, July 1998.

In Casa Alianza we are serious about defending children's human rights, and we have been taken seriously too, to the extent that one of our centres was attacked by machine-gun fire in Guatemala; three of our staff now live in Canada following death threats; and a Guatemalan judge sent us a court order of closure. Amnesty International has issued more than 35 world-wide Urgent Actions for Casa Alianza's children and staff. Personally, I am currently facing a five-year jail term for defamation – still considered a criminal rather than a civil offence in Guatemala – for daring to publicly name the wife of a high-ranking justice official for suspected participation in the international trafficking of children through international adoptions. Casa Alianza, together with the Attorney General's Office, have placed a total of eighteen criminal charges against lawyers in Guatemala for the trafficking of babies.

Since several Asian countries started to crack down on sex tourism in the late 1990s, couple of years ago, we have noticed a growing number of foreigners, almost exclusively males, coming to Central America – particularly Costa Rica and Honduras – to sexually abuse minors.

Since Casa Alianza's participation in the first World Congress against the Commercial Sexual Exploitation of Children, held in Stockholm in 1996, our legal aid offices have also started to focus on prosecuting those who commercially sexually exploit children, both pimps and clients. Our agency has also tried to win the commitment of the authorities of the affected countries. However, they often seem more concerned for the tourism image of their country than publicly recognizing that their countries have been targeted by paedophiles. Hence the need for efforts to stop the abuse of children.

To date, Casa Alianza has investigated and prosecuted sex tourists and other child abusers from Chile, Costa Rica, Germany, Guatemala, Honduras, Mexico, Sweden, Switzerland and the United States. In 1998, the Director of the Costa Rican Judicial Investigative Unit (OIJ) admitted that at least one half of one per cent of the close to one million foreign visitors to Costa Rica each year are so-called 'single sex tourists'. The former President of the Patronato Nacional de la Infancia, the Costa Rican Government's child welfare agency, admitted that 'there has been an accelerated increase in child prostitution' in the country. He further stated that '80 per cent of the children who prostitute themselves were sexually abused, often by their own family members'. This official blamed the increase in child sex tourism on promotion of Costa Rica on the Internet in both Europe and the United States. He agreed that unofficial estimates of more than 2,000 commercially sexually exploited children in the country with a total population of barely four million people 'could be scandalously higher'.

Even so, when Casa Alianza spoke with OIJ agents directly involved in the investigation of sex crimes in the country, none of them fully understood what the Internet was, nor did they have computers in their offices with which to access Internet. When we showed them some of the information available over the Internet about sex tourism in Costa Rica, they were truly shocked.

Legislation in the region

One of the major hurdles for Casa Alianza and the local authorities active in the prosecution of adults who sexually exploit children, is the fact that criminal laws in the region have not kept up with the changing forms of sexual exploitation of children. Throughout Central America, children are seen as objects 'owned' by their parents. Attempts to change attitudes to reflect the United Nations Convention on the Rights of the Child (ratified by all the countries in the region) often meet with strong resistance from some adults.

Examples of the inadequate laws with which we have to deal include Article 173 of the Criminal Code of Guatemala which considers the sexual abuse of a child as 'public' criminal rape only if the child victim is under the age of twelve. In this instance, anyone can report the crime, and the Public Prosecutor must investigate the case (the Public Prosecutor can also investigate ex-officio, i.e., without a formal complaint by the victim or a third party). If the child is twelve years old or over, sexual abuse, or rape, is considered to be a 'private' crime, i.e., only the victim or the parent or legal guardian of the child can report the crime. The same situation obtains in Article 140 of the Honduran Criminal Code (with the difference that the maximum age for the 'public' crime of rape is fourteen years).

Apart from having both weak and outdated laws, the legal systems in many Latin American countries are open to corruption. When foreigners are detained for a supposed crime, it is often possible to come to an extra-judicial 'understanding' with the arresting officer who earns perhaps US$300 a month. Corruption amongst judges is not uncommon either. Besides, it is generally the child who is detained as the criminal. If a man has been found guilty of raping an under-age girl, Article 200 of the Guatemalan Criminal Code allows for the waiving of the charges if the rapist agrees to marry the girl, provided she is aged over twelve. This is also the case in Honduras with Article 151 of the Criminal Code. These articles unfortunately leave the way open for payoffs, threats and other extra-judicial arrangements that generally do not consider what is best for the child victim.

There are no laws on the books in Central America at the time of writing regarding the possession of digital pornographic images, or downloading or sending them through the Internet. If the judicial authorities in Costa

Rica – the country in Central America with the highest number of Internet accounts per capita – have never surfed the Internet, one can readily imagine the even sadder situation in Honduras and Nicaragua. These countries need help. They are now being invaded by clever child sex abusers who know more about the Internet and how to use it to achieve their sordid goals than do the official investigative police bodies of those countries.

Perhaps the biggest problem is the lack of funding and training of many of the region's investigative police forces. The police are often little respected by the general public; they are underpaid and many are led to supplementing their income through corruption. There are some noteworthy exceptions to this sad state of affairs. Casa Alianza has found outstanding law enforcement officials in Costa Rica and Honduras who are equally frustrated by the weaknesses in both the laws and 'the system' in general. Even so, those who investigate and prosecute sex crimes in Central America are, so far as we have seen, generally unaware of the existence of extraterritorial laws when it comes to prosecuting foreign nationals for sex crimes against children in their country. These officials do not realize that an accused sex abuser of children can be deported directly to his home country for arrest and trial where the laws are generally stricter and the sentences enforced. Casa Alianza works closely with the United States Federal Bureau of Investigation (FBI) and with the Judicial Investigative Unit in Costa Rica in tracking and prosecuting offenders.

Chapter 20

CHILDREN AND THE LAW: THE CASE OF HONG KONG

Gordon Fung

Legislation on children giving evidence in criminal proceedings

In Hong Kong the law and procedures in respect of taking evidence in criminal proceedings can create difficulties for witnesses who are particularly vulnerable on account of their age, mental condition or fear of testifying. In various other jurisdictions, there have been changes to recognize the status of young children as witnesses and regulate the means by which children give evidence in criminal cases, either as victims of crime or as witnesses to crime.

Pursuant to recommendations made by various committees and working groups appointed to examine measures to make the criminal justice system more user-friendly, the government of Hong Kong amended the Evidence Ordinance and the Criminal Procedure Ordinance in 1995, in respect of the following categories of persons, who can be collectively described as vulnerable witnesses: children who have been sexually or physically abused; mentally handicapped persons; and witnesses in fear.

The new laws allow for children, the mentally handicapped and witnesses in fear to give evidence via a live television link; children and the mentally handicapped to give their evidence in chief on a video recording (with cross examination via a live television link); children under the age of fourteen to give unsworn evidence; the unsworn evidence of a child to be admitted without corroboration; and removal of the requirement that a jury must be warned of the danger of convicting an accused person on the uncorroborated evidence of a child.

Child abuse investigation

In response to the new legislation, the Hong Kong police set up five regional Child Abuse Investigation Units (CAIUs) in December 1995. They are augmented by a smaller Child Protection Policy Unit (CPPU). Recognizing that to protect the best interests of children needs standardized policies and working procedures, the government adopted a multidisciplinary approach to help victims of child abuse and their families. The Police and the Social Welfare Department also agreed to establish a joint investigation programme for child abuse cases. Police officers and social workers formed a Child Protection Special Investigation Team to investigate more serious cases of child sexual and physical abuse including: child sexual abuse where the victim is under the age of seventeen years and the alleged offender is a member of the family/extended family or known to the child; child sexual abuse involving multiple victims who are under the age of seventeen years; and serious child physical abuse where the victim is under the age of fourteen years. As well as conducting joint investigations with the Social Welfare Department, CAIUs assist other crime units in cases involving child and mentally handicapped victims and witnesses.

Interview suites

In order to provide a child-friendly environment for conducting videotaped interviews of child witnesses and victims, the Force has set up five interview suites away from police premises. These suites are all situated within residential blocks and are comfortably furnished. Children may relax by playing with toys in playhouses; reading storybooks or watching cartoons in a home-like environment prior to the interview. The suites are equipped with videorecording equipment and medical examination facilities for forensic medical examination of victims of child abuse.

The addresses of the suites are kept confidential to protect children from any intrusion by the media or offenders. The law also prohibits any media coverage that may lead to the identification of the victim in sexual abuse cases.

The Witness Support Programme

The Criminal Procedure Ordinance stipulates that a witness giving evidence through a live television link shall be accompanied by a person acceptable to the court, namely a support person. In November 1996, the Witness Support Programme was launched with the objective of providing emotional support and practical help for witnesses, to reduce the fear and anxiety that may arise when giving evidence in court. Trained non-government volunteers and family aides of the Social Welfare Department act as 'Support Persons'.

Apart from accompanying a child witness in court when giving evidence through the live television link, a support person will assist in the pre-trial preparation by explaining the role of a witness to the child. He or she will also accompany the child for a pre-trial familiarization visit to court. At the conclusion of the trial, the support person will inform the child of the case results. In the event of an acquittal, the support person would have to reassure the child that it was not his or her fault, and that the defendant was acquitted only because there was insufficient evidence.

> . . . the child shall in particular be provided the opportunity to be heard in any judicial and administrative proceedings affecting the child, either directly, or through a representative or an appropriate body, in a manner consistent with the procedural rules of national law. Article 12, United Nations Convention on the Rights of the Child.

Paedophiles and child pornography investigation

Paedophiles are often linked to the possession and distribution of child pornography. Intelligence on the activities of paedophiles comes mainly from overseas law enforcement agencies. Despite the limited information available in Hong Kong, there have been cases detected in relation to the publication of child pornography. Between May 1996 and November 1998, there were four cases involving the production of child pornographic materials by means other than the Internet. Three of these cases were brought to court and resulted in convictions. Sentences varied from fines to suspended imprisonment. There were five other cases of arrest involving publication of child pornographic materials on the Internet in the same period. Three of the cases resulted in convictions. As there is no legislation governing the production or distribution of child pornography, these cases were prosecuted under the Control of Obscene and Indecent Articles Ordinance.

The importance of information exchange with overseas law enforcement agencies is illustrated by the following case. Interpol Vienna supplied information on the publication of child pornography at two Internet addresses believed to be based in Hong Kong. As a result of police investigation, a man was arrested and charged with publishing an obscene article in 1997. He was convicted and sentenced to twenty-one months' imprisonment. His appeal, too, was dismissed.

Proposed legislation against child pornography and child sex tourism

In order to combat crimes against minors more effectively, in particular offences relating to child pornography, the Hong Kong government proposes to introduce new legislation to create offences of possession and/or distribution of child pornography, procurement or employment of children for child pornography, and advertisement of child pornography. In addition, the Hong Kong government proposes to provide current legislation against sexual abuse of children under the Crimes Ordinance with extraterritorial effect. Enactment of the new legislation will be another step forward and will mark Hong Kong's commitment to the United Nations Convention on the Rights of the Child.

Extradition and mutual legal assistance

At present, Hong Kong has signed extradition agreements with eleven countries. These are Australia, Canada, India, Indonesia, Malaysia, the Netherlands, New Zealand, the Philippines, Singapore, the United Kingdom and the United States. Hong Kong has also signed bilateral agreements on Mutual Legal Assistance with seven countries. These are Australia, France, Italy, New Zealand, the Republic of Korea, the United Kingdom and the United States. Agreements have been initialled with the Philippines and Switzerland. Such agreements allow for a wide range of assistance to be offered in the investigation and prosecution of criminal offences, for example, the service of documents, search and seizure, transfer of persons in custody to act as witnesses, or tracing, seizure and confiscation of the proceeds of crime.

POLICE OR SELF-POLICING: CAN THE INTERNET COMMUNITY DEAL WITH THE PROBLEM?

As is apparent from the preceding section, a purely 'crime and punishment' approach to controlling paedophilia and child pornography on the Internet is fraught with problems: constitutional, juridical, jurisdictional and technical. And given these problems, it is apparent that effective legal frameworks and enforcement mechanisms will take time to put in place. Yet clearly, something must be done, now and, in fact, is being done.

This section reviews actions by concerned citizens' groups, NGOs and the Internet 'industry' itself (service and content providers, telecommunications suppliers) to minimize, if not eliminate entirely, paedophilia and pornography on the Internet. These range from 'technical fixes' to cooperative efforts by parents' and other concerned user and industry groups to network, exchange information, monitor the Internet and report instances of abuse to the appropriate authorities and industry bodies. The media, which have played such an important role in bringing sexual abuse of children by child pornographers and paedophiles on the Internet to public attention, can also continue to contribute to controlling the problem.

Chapter 21

THE TECHNICAL RESPONSE: BLOCKING, FILTERING AND RATING THE INTERNET

Parry Aftab

Painting the entire Internet with a broad brush, complaining that it is primarily 'dangerous or objectionable material' is, of course, wrong. Although no one has reliable statistics, experts estimate that more than 90 per cent of the content of the Web is of general public interest, perfectly legal, and, if not necessarily educational or valuable, at least harmless. The remainder, however, generates far more traffic than the majority of the 90 per cent of harmless sites, and is seen by many parents, child custodians, teachers and by librarians as 'inappropriate for children'.

Understanding the situation, though, is only half of the job. Problems require solutions, or at least management. Some child protection advocates seek censorship and serious regulation of online content. Others lecture that any restrictions on freedom of speech, even by child caretakers and parents, are unacceptable and could indeed deprive children of access to valuable educational information. These two camps are better defined in the United States than in many other countries, simply because the Internet had been in use in the United States for longer than in most other countries. But the same debate is being heard throughout the world, as everyone tries to grapple with the difficult issues of managing content, censorship and safety.

No one disagrees that children should be kept safe: free from stalking and predators both online and offline, free from hate and 'cyberkid' marketing schemes, and free from exposure to adult materials and child pornography. But should this safety come at the expense of limiting adult access to what is not appropriate for a child? Is there an alternative to government regulations which censor 'speech' that is not appropriate for children? Is there a middle ground?

Rather than infringe on free speech, especially in the absence of a *universal* world standard, the solution would appear to be to empower parents, child custodians, teachers and librarians to make their own choice, by giving them the tools and services they need to apply in the way they deem most appropriate for their families, classrooms or libraries. By thinking creatively, and using this creativity to develop software tools, special services and Web projects, both adults and children can safely enjoy the Internet.

As the Internet population has grown, so too have products and services which address parents' concerns about appropriate and controlled Internet access for their children. These include filtering and blocking software products; server-based blocking and screening products; monitoring products which track where children have been online, as well as closed 'safe' intranet systems; rating systems; special child-safe search engines; parental controls; live-link 'spam' filters and more.

It should be noted though, that as parents and others gain more control over what their children can access, they limit more of the information that children can access, both good and bad, and they rely less on trust. This is the balance that each parent needs to strike, and their choices may differ child by child. There is no 'one size fits all' option when it comes to overseeing a child's Internet access. Each family has their own values, each child within the family needs a different level of protection and oversight, and children must be taught how to use their judgement online and to adhere to the rules of 'netiquette' which govern appropriate online behaviour. Not educating children about online risks and netiquette puts them at risk.

Of course, there is no way to make sure children that are 100 per cent protected from risks online (unless they are forever banned from using the Internet, which would be a terrible handicap to their future where all jobs are likely to require cyber-literacy). It should be recognized that everyone must accept some level of responsibility for safe surfing and that inevitably material will get through that a parent may wish had not. It is a risk everyone must learn to live with – to minimize and manage, but to learn to live with none the less. New products and services are introduced daily, but most of them fall into certain general types.

Filtering software

Since Net Nanny (then a Canadian company) introduced the first filtering product in January 1995, hundreds of filtering products have reached the market around the world. Filtering software products fall into several types. They either block 'bad' sites or only allow access to pre-approved 'good' sites. Most also filter words and phrases, and some even filter them in context to prevent blocking innocent phrases. Many also allow users to monitor and track where their children are going online, without blocking access.

Certain software can also monitor offline computer usage as well, such as how many hours (and which hours) the child spends on the computer or playing computer games. A few online services (such as America Online) provide their own proprietary products to members which work only on their systems. Some of the other software can be used with any of the online services (such as America Online, Prodigy, Compuserve and MSN), while others are designed only for the Internet itself.

Some software also blocks certain incoming information entirely, such as email, or filters incoming information. In addition, some prevent certain information from being sent by children to others (such as their name, address or telephone number). Online searches can be blocked or limited to child-friendly search engines (discussed below) as well, so children cannot search for undesirable sites.

The programs are either customizable or preset by the manufacturer of the software. Some allow users to set different levels of protection for different children, so restrictions for younger children can differ from those for their older siblings. Many of the better systems combine the various options, to give users the greatest protection and maximum flexibility.

In the United States where the issue of using filtering in libraries is now being tested for the first time, it is generally accepted among constitutional law experts that filtering all Internet access violates the First Amendment to the United States Constitution. No judicial guidance exists as to using filtering software on children's access, while allowing adults full unfiltered access. When libraries are included in this discussion of filtered access, such filtered access only relates to filtering children's access, while permitting adult unfettered Internet access.

Rating the Web: PICS (the Platform for Internet Content Selection)

In response to governmental and parental concerns regarding the amount and quality of content on the Internet, many of the leaders in the Internet and computer industries joined W3C (the World Wide Web Consortium) to create PICS (the Platform for Internet Content Selection). Often confused with a rating service, PICS is actually the technology which allows websites to carry ratings (which may be provided either by self-rating or third-party ratings services). PICS simply governs the format of the rating code and the way in which the codes are transmitted. It can be compared with a food product label regulation which specifies how large the text must to be, where on the product it should to appear and what colour the label has to be. Otherwise, the food product manufacturer labels its own product, just as the rating companies do.

Although many Internet industry actors were counting on PICS to be a serious solution for parents anxious to control their children's surfing, the rating services could not keep up with the explosive growth of the Web. This has damaged the chances of PICS-compliant ratings catching on globally. Even so, many still hope that ratings will catch on and become an additional tool for parents, educators and libraries.

> The very nature of the Internet poses limitations on the ability of service providers to block specified material particularly when there is no absolute way of knowing the full nature of the material, even if it is held within the jurisdiction. Blocking access to foreign websites represents a *particularly* difficult problem. From *Illegal and Harmful Use of the Internet*, Department of Justice, Equality and Law Reform, Dublin, July 1998.

The Recreational Software Advisory Council (RSAC) runs RSACi (RSAC on the Internet), a content-rating labelling system that rates sites on the Web. RSAC is the non-profit organization that developed a content-rating system for the level of violence contained in computer games. They have now taken their extensive experience and applied it to the Internet. RSACi uses a rating system to rate Internet sites for nudity, sexual content, violence and vulgarity.

Parents can select the types of content and levels of ratings appropriate for their children. As with movie ratings or food labels, parents become the informed decision-makers. Using content ratings allows parents, and not the online blockers or government censors, to decide what and how much their children should see.

The RSACi rating system has been available since 1 April 1996. There is no charge for obtaining a rating, and any website operator can submit a completed questionnaire at RSAC's website to obtain a rating label. The questionnaire asks a series of highly specific questions about the level, nature and intensity of offensive language and graphic content used on the site. The RSACi definitions can be consulted on the Internet. Although currently based on an honour system, where sites are trusted to accurately respond to the questionnaire, RSACi reserves the right to confirm the accuracy of the rating.

The RSAC server processes the questionnaire and produces HTML advisory tags which the website operator codes into the site. Web browsers then read these tags, permitting or blocking access to sites with specified ratings.

Most of the filtering products currently support the RSACi ratings system, and RSACi's ratings are the default standard for Microsoft's Internet Explorer. Netscape reports that it will be adding PICS support to its Netscape Navigator.

Search engine filters

Search engines allow Internet users to find particular sites, or sites about a certain topic. Among the popular ones are: AltaVista (which contains a translating feature to translate sites from one language to another), Excite, Infoseek, Lycos, and Yahoo! Although some search engines hire people to visit the sites and categorize them into directories, most search engines use robot software (called bots, spiders and crawlers). These devices scour the Web searching every word at every website, and in some cases, all pages linked to those sites. It then indexes all those sites, based upon the number of search words used and how often they are used within the site.

Webmasters, in order to make sure that the 'spiders' index their sites, properly use hidden code, called 'meta-tags', to list the keywords they want the search engine to use to categorize their sites. For example, the UNESCO site might use the name 'United Nations' in its meta-tags, so people searching for the United Nations' site will also see that of UNESCO, or it may use 'educational, scientific and cultural' or 'NGO' in its tags.

Some unscrupulous webmasters, in order to drive traffic to their sites, will use meta-tag keywords that do not properly categorize the site. For example, they may use the word 'sex' in their meta-tags, so that people who are searching for sex sites might visit theirs, even though they are selling something else. So too do they use popular children's topics and character names in their meta-tags to drive traffic to their sites. For example (and notwithstanding infringement of trademarks or copyright) a sex site may use the name 'Disney' or 'Nickelodeon' in their meta-tags, since these are very popular search items. Even if the site visitor immediately leaves the site when learning of its real nature, that visitor will count towards the number of 'hits' the site receives, and will affect advertising rates for the site's advertisers.

Unscrupulous webmasters may also use domain names which are intended to confuse surfers. For example, one could use names of known government entities or institutions, to make the surfer think he is going to a government site, but instead of using the normal suffix 'gov' one might use 'com' or 'net' or other, and the actual site may have nothing to do with the government but instead portray salacious images. The surfer is then led to believe that these images originated from a government source and that government condones such portrayals. The 'name of the game' is advertising revenue, and these webmasters will do whatever they can to increase site traffic, even if it means misleading children. While filtering software may avoid some of these situations, most search engines turn up inappropriate sites when innocent searches are executed. That is why some search engines, concerned about adult content being accessible to children, have set up special search engine sites just for children.

The most popular child-oriented and filtered English-language search engines are: Yahooligans!, Ask Jeeves for Kids and DIG (Disney's search engine). The number of sites available are necessarily limited, and some of the sites may be dressed-up advertisements, but the likelihood of running across inappropriate adult material is very small. Real people (not bots) review all DIG and Yahooligans! sites to make sure that they are appropriate for children, while Ask Jeeves for Kids relies on a filtering software to screen out inappropriate material.

Note that filtered search engines are not intended to function as a substitute for Internet safety education, parental supervision or parental control software, nor are they foolproof. For example, while a search for an R-rated movie may be blocked, the link to movie-related sites may give children information about such movies.

Many schools are developing closed systems, with the commercial market following their lead. These are dial-in or local server products, and do not use the Internet or provide access to the Internet. Many are optimistic that the growth of entertaining and educational content online will give children safe alternatives to adult and inappropriate content for children and will calm the concerns of parents, educators and librarians.

By working together, the world-wide Internet community can find solutions to these problems and guarantee our children a fun, safe and entertaining surfing adventure.

Chapter 22

THE INDUSTRY RESPONSE 1: THE INTERNET INDUSTRY AND ILLEGAL CONTENT

Jean-Christophe Le Toquin

Established on 10 September 1997, 'Eurolspa' groups European Internet service providers associations. Its membership is drawn from ten countries: Austria, Belgium, Finland, France, Germany, Ireland, Italy, the Netherlands, Spain and the United Kingdom, representing in total some 500 service providers. The issue of illegal content transmitted via the Internet is one of Eurolspa's primary concerns.

The Internet, a specific communication space

The Internet is a communication space characterized by a varied range of services and functions, using very diverse techniques in a multimedia mode (telecommunications, computing and audio-visual). This makes it possible for different players to provide different services, the main ones being email, newsgroups and Websites. The most striking features of these services are the wide diversity of content they offer (commercial services, copyright-protected works, news articles, etc.) and the variety of potential audiences (e.g., a general audience, a particular audience segment or a particular individual).

Regarding functions

The functions performed vary, depending on whether the player is a user or service provider offering infrastructure, access, host or content services. In terms of responsibility, a distinction must be made between the provision of purely technical services, like access and host services, and the provision of content, such as Website management.

A further distinction must be kept in mind between the activities of Internet service providers, which consist of allowing users to access content that the service provider has no hand in, and the activities of commercial online providers, which consists of giving users access to content put online by the online provider itself or by independent third parties subject to agreement.

The preceding analysis is made more complex by the fact that any one player can perform several functions. The Internet is set apart from other modes of communication by the participatory options it makes available to players. Any person, private or professional, who connects to the Internet, can receive and/or issue and/or transmit information, either for a fee or free of charge. In practical terms, this means than all users have the possibility to both retrieve and put information online.

The Internet is set apart from other modes of communication by its world-wide, network-based structure. It forms a network of networks that is global, and no longer national, in scope. This means that if a site cannot be accessed by one particular path, an alternative route will be found. Similarly, if one server is closed down, the same data can be made accessible using another server, which may be located in another country, for example. Within the framework of an open and international structure, it is difficult to pinpoint the exact location of data and control its distribution. Thus, except in the case of purely national disputes, efforts should be made to devise a mode of regulation making international coordination of national regulations possible. However, regulation of Internet content and services by a central body and, *a fortiori*, by national legislation, is not adequate. This finding is shared by all the relevant reports produced to date by such bodies as the OECD or the European Union.

It is striking to note that, at the present time, almost all the European countries and the United States have chosen not to enact national legislation for the Internet, opting instead for self-regulation through hotline systems. The Internet is set apart from other modes of communication by the difficulty in distinguishing between public and private communication, and in knowing at what point, and according to what criteria, a private meeting can be considered public.

To this difficulty is added the constant evolution of transmission techniques, which sometimes undermines accepted definitions. Thus, 'push' transmission techniques, which make it possible to send information automatically (public transmission) in line with users' predetermined requests (private demand), makes it all the more difficult to draw the line between public and private. Sending electronic mail using collective mailing lists raises the same difficulties. Depending on their popularity, accessibility or the audience targeted, discussion groups, discussions on an IRC, mailing lists, and even Web sites, can be classified as either private or public.

The Internet is also set apart from other modes of communication by its instantaneity. On the Internet, putting data online or sending written messages can produce immediate effects in the same way as if they were transmitted orally. Discussion groups are an excellent illustration of this. Messages are written and remain retrievable for several days. However, the tone and rapidity of the exchanges is often reminiscent of a conversation, with its interplay of questions and answers, in a mode that is for the most part spontaneous.

The Internet is an innovative mode of communication in that it combines the power of the written word with the rapidity of the spoken word on a planetwide scale. Within a communication space as original as the Internet, dealing with the issue of illegal content requires a specifically tailored response.

The Internet and illegal content

Both national and international public authorities understand the importance of the new space created by the Internet. They support its development, while remaining aware of the difficulties it poses. Indeed, the Internet is a communication space through which data, of all kinds and from all sources, transit, some of which may be illegal. The concept of what is legal or illegal may vary from country to country, but society generally recognizes the need to defend certain universal values, including the protection of children and human dignity.

To defend these essential values, pragmatism and cooperation among all players based on shared principles, are today considered the best principles on which to build an appropriate response to the difficulties posed by the Internet without curtailing its advantages.

These principles underpin the action of Eurolspa and its members.

> We believe it is not only impossible but also counterproductive to attempt to 'regulate' the Internet in the sense of introducing new national statutory provisions to specifically control its illegal and harmful use. . . This is not to say that our national laws should not continue to take careful cognisance of the emerging technology; 'Internet proofing' of new legislation is among our recommendations. From *Illegal and Harmful Use of the Internet,* Department of Justice, Equality and Law Reform, Dublin, July 1998.

Codes of conduct and contact points

In addition to those noted above, other forms of regulation must be promoted, such as the establishment of codes of conduct and contact points. A number of Eurolspa members have already put in place national codes of conduct.

A number of service providers' associations have also set up Internet sites dedicated specifically to reporting illegal content of a paedophile nature or incitement to racial hatred. These sites are intended to assist net users faced with suspected illegal content in finding a contact point at which to file their complaint.

On a case-by-case basis, these contact points either deal with claims directly (by establishing contact with the site administrator, the service provider, the police, etc.) or refer net users to the competent companies or services. Alone or in partnership with other national associations, the members of Eurolspa have already developed a number of these initiatives. Each site has its own mode of functioning and funding, depending on the sensitivity of the national structures, with the full respect and knowledge of the other initiatives.

European service providers are already cooperating with each other to find a solution to the issue of illegal content, which will not impinge on the benefits of the information society. The Internet Action Plan being prepared by the European Commission will serve as a useful tool in coordinating and pursuing the development of these actions. Broader-based international initiatives such as the UNESCO Declaration and Action Plan on Child Pornography and Paedophilia on the Internet initiative will undoubtedly also make a very significant contribution to the process.

Chapter 23

THE INDUSTRY RESPONSE 2: SELF-REGULATION BY THE INTERNET INDUSTRY

David Kerr

In Europe, the Internet Watch Foundation (IWF) in the United Kingdom is one of the first attempts at self-regulation of illegal and offensive content by the Internet industry itself.

Although action is required to remove illegal content from the Internet, attention is focusing increasingly on the ways in which children can be barred from accessing Internet material which their parents or teachers may consider harmful. This kind of material, although it might be considered as pornographic by the public at large, may be legal under relevant legislation, even if it is classified as potentially harmful under the terms of, for example, the European Commission Communication on Illegal and Harmful Content or the United States Child Online Protection Act. Latest research by the IWF shows that many potential users of the Internet fear subscribing as they do not know what they may be letting into their homes, and if connected, new users show a strong desire for a means of filtering what they or their children can see.

> While the determination of illegal use is complicated, final decisions on legality in any given jurisdiction are determined by due legal process. Harmful use of the Internet is a much more subjective issue. What is considered harmful can vary between countries and indeed, within a particular country. It is sometimes a matter of taste, culture and value systems, and is very much dependent on whether or not children are involved. From *Illegal and Harmful Use of the Internet*, Department of Justice, Equality and Law Reform, Dublin, July 1998.

Thus, controlling harmful content is a major issue for protecting children as well as identifying, investigating and prosecuting the originators of illegal material.

Self-regulation

'Self-regulation' is perhaps a misnomer for the United Kingdom approach as although the industry funds and supports the IWF, its operation is founded on a joint agreement between government, police and industry. Like any partnership it survives and succeeds because it continues to provide demonstrable benefits to all the participants.

However, in a global medium, the IWF's effectiveness depends on extending the partnership between the private and public sectors in the global arena. Hence the value of international meetings such as those sponsored by UNESCO.

Illegal material

The IWF's primary role in the United Kingdom was to establish a hotline for the public to report illegal material. Internet service providers (ISPs) can and do remove illegal material from their United Kingdom servers. Links between the ISPs and the police help to get originators of illegal content, primarily child pornography, investigated and prosecuted. Despite this, since an estimated 95 per cent of the originators are based outside the United Kingdom, a truly effective response depends on similar arrangements in other countries.

This is already happening: there are now other hotlines operating in Europe and in the United States, and plans for many more – in Australia, Europe and Japan. The European Union's action plan for promoting safe use of the Internet is encouraging the growth of hotlines and helping to build them into an international network.

Legal but potentially harmful material

Useful as hotlines are, it has to be accepted that they will never eradicate illegal material or do anything about the swathe of legal material that many people will find objectionable, and from which they would want to protect their children.

This is where IWF's second role in developing rating and filtering techniques comes to the fore. After extensive research and debate, most governments and much of the industry has accepted that this approach is the best hope for maintaining free speech on the Internet, whilst providing the means for consumers to choose what they do not wish to see.

The rationale of the IWF approach in the United Kingdom presents another of the enigmas of the Internet. The IWF's primary interest, like any other national body, is in the needs of the country. But the only way that the needs of United Kingdom residents and businesses can be well served is by an international endeavour. The rating approach needs a critical mass of sites rated in a way that United Kingdom-based browsers can interpret, and according to the categories of content that the United Kingdom public wishes to filter. The need is the same in other countries. Thus, for a world-wide rating system to work, it needs to be culturally neutral so that each user may apply their individual standards and national culture. It needs to be simple and cheap to install and operate. Technically less sophisticated parents need to be able to set it up for their more technologically up-to-date off-spring. Content providers must be able to rate their sites easily and quickly.

This specification sounds a tall order! But systems are already running that can do it, notably the RSACi system, which recently won the Carl Bertelsmann prize for innovation and responsibility in the information society.

The IWF is currently working with RSAC and others, to establish a truly universal rating and filtering system, which takes account of the requirements of all Internet users, wherever they live. This is through the Internet Content Rating Alliance. In order to take into account the particular needs of all countries and cultures in the build-up to specifying this system, the IWF has formed an International Reference Group, which will be consulting stakeholders world-wide on their requirements for a global system. The IWF has been currently actively recruiting international participants for the Reference Group which held its first meeting in October 1998. The IWF's programme has been promised European Commission funding and is also seeking sponsorship from Internet industries worldwide. The IWF's intention was to have the system operational by the end of 1999.

Conclusions

To make such a system truly international requires a global partnership effort between governments and industry: governments to support the process of identifying the particular requirements of their citizens while staying 'hands-off' to reduce fears of state censorship; the Internet industry to advance the browser technology and encourage subscribers to install and use the systems available; the content industry to recognize the mutual benefits of cooperation and the commercial advantages of rating their sites.

Chapter 24

THE ACADEMIC AND RESEARCH RESPONSE 1: A RESEARCH AND CIVIC INITIATIVE IN BELGIUM

Béatrice van Bastelaer

At the beginning of September 1996, following the public uproar aroused by a particularly sensational paedophilia case (the Dutroux affair), several researchers and academics at the University of Notre-Dame de la Paix in Namur, Belgium, decided to set up the MAPI Group (Anti-Paedophilia Movement on the Internet). This study group focused primarily on the presence of information on the Internet inciting the sexual exploitation of children and launched a programme of research on the subject.

Many people, ranging from researchers to typical net-surfers, as well as parents, indicated their wish to contribute to our work. Some provided us with useful information or names of associations likely to help us move forward. Others promised to actively participate in the research, or simply to support us by showing our logo in their respective websites.

> We can serve humanity or destroy it. But whatever destroys our children destroys us. Homayra Sellier, President of the World Citizens' Movement to Protect Innocence in Danger.

For eight months MAPI held fortnightly meetings. During that period we studied the problems relating to the dissemination of information on the Internet inciting the sexual exploitation of children, as well as the currently available and potential technical solutions to those who did not want to be exposed to this kind information. We created a questionnaire aimed at Internet service providers to learn their position on the matter. We also studied the present state of Belgian law as well as legal mechanisms instituted by other countries. In addition, we also studied alternative solutions concerning child paedophilia on the Internet, involving the Internet as a medium and its specific rules of operation.

Our first major activity ended in March 1997 with the publication of a report and the organization of a public conference at which the findings of the research were presented and discussed. The report is available on the MAPI website, and consists of five chapters: *To Understand* gives a definition of child pornography and a description of the Internet; *To Deepen* describes the various types of information on the Internet including that which incites the sexual exploitation of children, and presents the results of the survey on the attitude of the Belgian Internet service providers vis-à-vis the problem of paedophilia on the Internet; *To Regulate* suggests technical, legal and ethical solutions; *To Act* proposes concrete actions for Internet users that would enable them to contribute to MAPI activities and make Internet users aware of the presence of paedophilia-oriented information on the Internet and encourage them users to react when confronted with this type of information; *To Reflect* gives the basis of a deeper understanding about liberties on the Internet, and on the necessity to reject (to react) rather than to prohibit (to regulate).

The public conference organized in March 1997, involving a wide range of personalities concerned by and working with the Internet in Belgium, reached the following conclusions:

1. The Internet represents very specific problems: first, the ease with which child pornography can spread on the network compared to the more traditional channels of dissemination; second, the 'virtual' existence of paedophiles, much more isolated in the past, but who now can find one another and group together using the Internet;

2. Some have attempted to determine the quantity of information inciting sexual exploitation of children on the Internet. However, regardless of the precise amount of paedophilia-oriented information existing on the Internet, what is important is what society can accept or tolerate. The volume of information is not the main point. Contrary to what is often heard, it is *not* necessary to change the law to adapt it to the specific case of the Internet: what is 'illegal' in conventional media is also illegal on the Net, and criminal law concerning child pornography is equally applicable to the Internet. There seems to be a tendency to react more severely with regard to the Internet relative to traditional sources of child pornography, often without fully measuring the consequences of the solutions advocated. The specificity of the Internet is the problem of jurisdiction, notably when pornographic or paedophilic information is sourced in a foreign country.

3. It is necessary to make *all* Internet actors aware of their responsibilities, both the users and the Internet industry, particularly the service providers. The latter often tend to hide behind technical and financial constraints that allegedly make it difficult for them to know the nature of the information they have on their servers – yet they are able to 'clean up' some of their content according to criteria of their own choice. Therefore, it is necessary that users should be better informed about these criteria as well as the laws in force, and that service providers seek the cooperation of their users in the fight against this illegal information.

Finally, all the solutions considered during the conference and in the MAPI report, i.e., technical and legal solutions, self-regulation and building awareness among users, are partial responses which must be set to work in complementarity with each other.

> The challenge for education is two-fold. First, how can the educational system, working in synergy with other social institutions, become a proactive force for social change? The aim of this collaboration is to ensure a change in attitude and practice by all social institutions and systems that will engender protection, respect and promotion of the humanity, dignity and rights of children. Second, how can the educational system counteract the negative impact and reinforce the empowering and enabling lessons of informal learning? Formal or non formal educational programmes are not sufficient as they stand, even for those children who are already attending school. Education is not a panacea, nor will educational measures alone suffice to combat the depredation of children in the sex trade. At the same time, no effort to address the problem will be *workable or sustainable* without them. 'Education: The Motor of Change', background paper edited by Manzoor Ahmed and Sara Ann Friedman for the World Congress against Commercial Sexual Exploitation of Children.

To conclude, while MAPI has concerned itself with Internet material conveying child pornography, the Belgian Criminal Investigation Department, and especially its section dealing with Internet questions, has been concerned with persons, i.e., paedophiles. The most important thing is that paedophiles and their activities be stopped. The dissemination of images of child pornography is a consequence of paedophilic activities, and not a cause. Even so, it is necessary to prevent their propagation which can only tend to normalize paedophilia and child pornography. Behind these images, we should not forget, there are often children – and adults – who are suffering. At the end of the conference, all the participants underlined the need to grant sufficient means to those who are fighting paedophilia and child pornography 'in the real world', that is, the legal authorities and associations.

MAPI continues to receive messages denouncing litigious sites and requests for assistance to counteract this type of material. In all cases, we immediately forward these requests to the Belgian Criminal Investigation

Department. It is important to note that very often, associations like MAPI play an essential 'mailbox' role between the concerned public and law enforcement agencies. Denunciation to the police remains something psychologically difficult for many people and an independent and neutral 'hotline' serves a very essential role in this respect.

Thus, organizations such as MAPI are important as they fulfil three missions: they make the public aware of the problem through a constantly updated Website; they provide technical and scientific information to those who ask for more targeted data (how to counterattack; what is the real efficiency of the filters; what filter to use; what is the real value of self-regulation; what are the dangers of censorship, etc.) and to continue the search for practical and efficient solutions; and they act as a relay between the Internet users and the legal authorities.

Chapter 25

THE ACADEMIC AND RESEARCH RESPONSE 2: RESEARCH AND COOPERATION

Jo Groebel

The problem

While the topic of children as consumers of violent media has a long scientific tradition, it is only recently that attention has also turned to children as *victims* of on-screen violence. Now, the discovery of tens of thousands of graphic images of abused, tortured or even murdered children have created the will to take some action towards prevention.

Analysis

Child pornography has been around since the creation of visual media. However, the Internet – given its global character – now offers much easier, anonymous access without the immediate threat of prosecution as often was the case where other media were used. Of course, the Internet is not the problem *per se*. It offers many constructive possibilities for information and communication flows, but does pose specific social risks as is often the case with other new technologies.

> Moral panic based on poor understanding of the Internet is an enemy to progress. Awareness is a key part of any overall national strategy in this are. . . .
> From *Illegal and Harmful Use of the Internet*, Department of Justice, Equality and Law Reform, Dublin, July 1998.

These risks, more specifically, are the following: the Internet facilitates the operation of an international underground market for child pornography, additionally many adults who normally would not be interested in child pornography via other vehicles become interested in the subject out of curiosity and thrill-seeking, because of the ease of access and anonymity of the Net. Children, on the other hand, are not normally *consumers* of child pornography, even when confronted with this material, but may either become traumatized or habituated to graphic child pornography. In both cases, the group of potential users is extended beyond traditional pornographic circles, and with the high attention and increased interest in the issue, even legitimate media may become involved, e.g., by 'flirting' with child pornography in advertisements, creating 'ambivalent' images where adult models pose as children, and so on.

To the extent that one can draw a parallel with markets, children become potential 'sexual sales products'. Children as victims are particularly at risk in two facets of this 'market': as an exchange product *within* child pornography circles (families, friends, etc.), and as a trade product similar to prostitution where they are 'sold' for cash. While both forms of 'marketing' are subject to criminal law prosecution, the latter case (international trade) would seem to call for the specific attention of a global organization.

Possible solutions

There is sufficient media-effects research to identify the risk potential (see the UNESCO Global Media Violence Study, Groebel, 1998, and the UNESCO Clearing House, Sweden). However, more research should be devoted to the international aspects of the problem: what is the international distribution of this phenomenon? How do different national laws and policies deal with the problem? What is the global flow of images, of children as 'trade products', and what forms does this trade take? Under what circumstances (economic, cultural, tourism) do children in particular risk becoming victims of child pornography? The analysis should here compare the links within criminal circles operating in other forms of trade (e.g., the link with prostitution). Most of all, are there any successful preventive measures, apart from legal prosecution, which can contribute to the solution of the problem, e.g., media education, parent information, and so forth?

> Challenges to any study of international child pornography include: 1) the lack of any uniform definition of what child pornography entails; 2) lack of data regarding the production and distribution of child pornography in many parts of the world, particularly Africa and Latin America; and 3) shifting global patterns of production and consumption of child pornography. Margaret A. Healy, 'Child Pornography: An International Perspective', paper prepared for the World Congress against Commercial Sexual Exploitation of Children.

We suggest than an existing institution with some expertise in child issues be asked to systematically gather, structure and communicate information in the above-mentioned areas on an international level. There are, surely, still questions that remain unanswered, like the international trade aspect of the problem. These could be analyzed in a medium-sized research study, e.g., with cooperation between UNESCO, the UNESCO Clearing House at Gothenberg University, and Utrecht University.

Most of all, it is crucial to immediately link the conclusions of existing and future analyses with positive suggestions for action, e.g., educative and communicative. In particular, UNESCO should play a central role in developing international information/communication policy regarding the problem, as well as the necessary educative measures in schools and with parents. In addition, UNESCO should contribute to international awareness of the problem at the level of governments and institutions. Here, there is perhaps a special role for women who are key international opinion-leaders and who could be asked to serve as 'ambassadors' in combating child pornography and paedophilia on the Internet.

Chapter 26

THE MEDIA RESPONSE: A JOURNALIST'S VIEW OF THE PROBLEM IN ASIA

Carol Aloysius

A little more than a decade ago, if I were asked, 'Is sexual abuse of children a serious problem in Sri Lanka?' my answer would have been negative. Today of course, we know differently. This is due in no small measure to an awareness-raising campaign by a Sri Lankan NGO, the Organisation Protecting Environment and Children Everywhere (PEACE). It was a study by PEACE that shocked Sri Lankan society as a whole into realizing that, far from being a haven for tourists in search of the sun and golden beaches, our country was also attracting an unsavoury tribe of tourists – the paedophiles who came here solely to gratify their sexual needs for young children.

The scenario is similar in other Asian countries too, including Burma, Cambodia, India, Nepal, Pakistan and Thailand, wherever poverty exists in its extreme forms, and where the tourist industry has expanded exponentially, often with government support in order to bring much-needed revenue into these countries. In all these countries (most of whom have ratified the Convention on the Rights of the Child adopted by the United Nations in 1989), child prostitution and the commercial sexual exploitation of children have grown to unprecedented levels in recent years, largely as a result of a developing economy and an expanding tourist industry. So much so, that today an international organization has been formed, called ECPAT (End Child Prostitution in Asian Tourism).

To give some idea of the magnitude of the problem in the Asian region alone, a senior judge in Sri Lanka, at a seminar on child abuse was quoted as saying that there are an estimated 500,000 prostitutes aged 16 years and younger in Thailand, 400,000 in India, 30,000 boy prostitutes in Sri Lanka,

100,000 in the Philippines and another 100,000 in Taiwan. This report also claims that in other countries such as Nepal, Pakistan and Vietnam, child prostitution is also widely prevalent, while in Burma, Cambodia, Indonesia and Laos and some provinces of China, children are being trafficked across borders for the purpose of serving in brothels.

Some of these countries have challenged the accuracy of the statistics, charging that they are exaggerated, while in other countries it is alleged that politicians and NGOs with vested interests have exaggerated the figures to suit their interests. However, while these charges may be true to some extent, one thing is certain: it is clear from emerging evidence that the menace of child sexual abuse is now very much a widespread phenomenon in the Asian region as a whole.

> The underlying causes are numerous, and include: economic injustice and result-
> ing disparities between rich and poor, large-scale migration and urbanization, fam-
> ily disintegration. They include historic and continuing cultural values which
> discriminate against girls and women, the influx of materialist values and goods,
> perpetrated by the media, and the subsequent deterioration of traditional commu-
> nity and cultural support systems. Ignorance certainly plays a role in the commer-
> cial sexual exploitation of children but is something that can be remedied. In
> particular, educating parents on the fate of their children sold into labour, bondage
> and sex, would reduce the numbers of parents willing to even consider such sale. In
> some parts of the world, such as Nepal, local community groups are working with
> the press and media to show parents what can happen when they deliver their chil-
> dren into the hands of an agent who promises money and a better life. World Con-
> gress against Commercial Sexual Exploitation of Children: Contributing Factors.

What has caused the proliferation of this horrendous evil in the Asian region in particular? Certainly, one of the reasons is the spread of tourism. Although there may be a certain percentage of tourists who certainly come for paedophile activities, not all tourists who visit Sri Lanka do so.

What has happened is that in most Asian countries, opening up to tourists has also made them vulnerable to paedophile rings operating world-wide. Closely linked to this is poverty, and the desperate need to make ends meet, that has driven parents to selling their own children to foreign pae-dophiles in order to keep the home fires burning.

There is no doubt that in Asia and other countries where child prostitution is prevalent, the victims come from the poorest of the poor. They are either sold to pimps and peddlers of flesh or induced to sell their bodies against their will, because of their abject poverty. It is no secret that many of the victims are unprotected children, such as street children, for whom quick money, even a negligible amount, and a few luring presents such as a bar of chocolate or candy or ball-point pens make them easy prey, especially to paedophiles.

However, poverty is not the only reason why children fall victims to pae-dophilia. Parents must also take the blame, for many of these children lack adult supervision. Many of them do go to school, but from there run out and wander without their parents knowledge. Their parents are either away from home until late at night, do not see the importance of supervising their children's movements, or are too busy with their own affairs. The ignorance of parents of the very real dangers of allowing their children to be sexually abused is another reason why so many young children are given the green light to join the world's oldest profession in this part of the world.

To cite an often-quoted statement by a father when asked by a social worker in Sri Lanka why he allowed his teenage son to be abused by foreign paedophiles, 'My son cannot get pregnant. So what does it matter since he brings in much needed cash?' Little did this same father realize that his son would end up with Aids and eventually succumb to the disease.

Child pornography in Asian countries and on the Internet: the role of the media

Another reason for the flood of paedophiles to Asian countries is the prolific growth in the availability of child pornographic material in video parlours and on the Internet, much of which has originated in this part of the world, i.e., the Philippines, Sri Lanka and Thailand, to name but a few countries. In recent years, this problem has escalated sharply in South Asia, where it is believed that there are as many as one million children under 15 years who are in prostitution and selling their bodies for sex or for pornographic films. This has caused grave concern to child activists, who are now calling for help from the media to combat this menace.

The response from the media has been positive and encouraging, to say the least, and all over Asia the media have used various strategies to halt this widespread abuse of children. One very effective strategy has been an awareness-raising campaign to alert the public to the number of young boys and girls, some as young as eight, being used as models in pornographic films to whet the sexual appetites of paedophiles looking for new prey.

Across Asia, notably in India, the Philippines and Thailand, wherever governments too have committed themselves to combating child abuse in all forms, the media have joined hands with them, the NGOs and the police to eradicate this menace to society.

Certain sections of the media have gone a step further than merely carrying out awareness campaigns. They have offered to help investigate some cases brought to their attention, taking on a quasi-police role. A privately owned Sri Lankan newspaper started a hotline on child abuse, and also volunteered to send out reporters to investigate cases if no one else came forward to do so. It is this kind of innovative action that is needed we need to make the media play a more meaningful role in the war against child sexual abuse in Asia.

Apart from pornographic material which one can discreetly view at a video parlour or borrow to watch in the privacy of one's own home, child pornography on the Internet has become one of the most grave problems and challenges that face Asian societies today.

The phenomenon came to light recently because the Internet itself has expanded so rapidly in the last decade. It has gone from being an obscure resource used occasionally by academics, to becoming a mass medium used by approximately 100 million people across the world. The figure, we are told, is growing every day. Worse still, it has become a place where sexual perverts, such as paedophiles and child pornographers, go to look for their victims. Asian children make up the bulk of these.

In Sri Lanka, a high-ranking official from a government department dealing with child care allegedly admitted that there were at least 600 Sri Lankan boy children who are regularly advertised on the Internet, with detailed descriptions of their bodies, by providers of pornographic material requested by paedophiles.

With no stiff penalties to deter them from their activities until recent amendments to the penal code, making child pornographic films was a lucrative and flourishing business in Sri Lanka. It is only now, with the passing of a new law against obscene publications involving children, that there seems to be a lull in this once lucrative trade. Or has it merely gone underground?

The role of the media in preventing child pornography

Why do Asian children form the bulk of victims of child pornographic material on the Internet as well as on videos that are watched daily either in video parlours or behind closed doors? What makes them such easy prey to paedophiles from other countries who come specially to these developing nations looking for victims whose names, addresses and sex organs have been described in detail on the Internet? How can the media act as a sentinel, a watchdog, and prevent such pornographic material from appearing on the Internet? These are questions that the Asian media must address in future.

The Internet is a recent phenomenon in the Asian region. In Sri Lanka there are less than ten thousand users of the Internet because it is still beyond the reach of the average person due to high costs. Still, in the new millennium, it is likely to spread. Facing this prospect, the media must be alert; report findings of pornographic material on the Internet (avoiding graphic details so as not to rouse the desires of child abusers); and caution parents of high-risk children who could become the victims of child pornographers.

One of the most effective strategies – apart from creating general awareness among the public – would be to win the commitment of political leaders to this cause. If change is to come about in laws protecting children from such abuse, then there must be political commitment. This is happening right now in many countries of South Asia, where the media are carrying out a sustained campaign to protect children at risk, with encouraging results.

Shortcomings on the part of the media

There are however, some negative factors we have to consider with regard to the Asian media, which has been sometimes accused of not being sensitive to child abuse issues. The media have been accused of not being well informed, of not researching the facts and statistics given to them, of covering issues related to child abuse in an irresponsible manner and of jeopardizing the child victim rather than protecting him or her.

In reply to the charge that the Asian media sometimes superficially covers issues on child abuse, it should be said that this is not deliberate. The Asian media are also limited by a lack of full-time specialists in the field of child abuse (few newspapers in the Asian region can afford the luxury of employing full-time child abuse correspondents) and are therefore not in a position to critically evaluate whatever information they receive.

The Asian media have also been accused of failing to query the sources from which they receive statistics and information, and aligning themselves with NGOs with ostensibly vested interests, who are mostly donor-aided and are thus merely echoing the sentiments of their donor agencies.

It is thus up to the media to be ever alert when reporting child sexual abuse cases and they must guard against vested interests and hidden agendas on the part of various NGOs involved in such campaigns. They must try to infuse balance and objectivity into their reporting.

> States Parties recognize the important function performed by the mass media and shall ensure that the child has access to information and material from a diversity of national and international sources, especially those aimed at the promotion of his or her social, spiritual and moral well-being and physical and mental health. Article 17, United Nations Convention on the Rights of the Child.

In spite of these shortcomings, the Asian media have great potential in helping to combat child abuse in the region as a whole. In Asian countries where the media often play the multiple roles of being the first informant, commentator and guide, they can play a very powerful role in combating sexual abuse of children.

At the beginning of the new millennium, the most formidable challenge for the media both in Asia and other parts of the world is child pornography on the Internet. The Asian media, which are just now beginning to exploit the benefits of the Internet, should be ever alert and vigilant to child pornography and should educate the public, monitor service providers and inform the police when such material is brought to its notice. If, on the other hand, the media simply sit back and do nothing, they would be passive accomplices to a grievous wrong being done to the thousands of hapless child victims already trapped in this evil web. I believe that workshops and seminars at regional level can help media personnel to exchange ideas on common problems and work out more effective solutions for their respective countries.

Chapter 27

An NGO response: ECPAT International's strategy

Muireann O'Briain

ECPAT International

The ECPAT (End Child Prostitution, Child Pornography and Trafficking of Children for Sexual Purposes) mandate is to combat child prostitution, child pornography and trafficking in children for sexual purposes. We are a campaigning organization, seeking to address the issues through leadership and the promotion of ideas of partnership and good practice. While we do have some grass-roots projects and assist training in recovery and reintegration of victims, the biggest thrust of our work is to get national governments to put in place adequate protection systems against sexual exploitation of children and to empower local groups to combat the problem.

Combating child pornography on the Internet

In Europe, ECPAT groups have begun to tackle the problem of child pornography on the Internet. They have worked to develop the use and coordination of hotlines for reporting of child pornography and to raise awareness among parents and children of the dangers on the Net.

> We must make a qualitative leap for the protection of our children. Her Royal Highness Princess Maria Teresa of Luxembourg, UNESCO Ambassador of Good Will.

ECPAT International organized, along with Interpol, an Expert Meeting on Child Pornography on the Internet in May 1998 at which service providers, law enforcers and non-governmental organizations discussed the actions already being taken and the possibilities for a more global, coordinated response to the phenomenon. Suggestions for further action arising from that meeting included: the creation of multi-agency law enforcement agencies; support for the work of the Interpol Standing Working Party on Offences against Minors and its resource list of training courses and proper resources for law enforcement in general; standardization of ISP transactional records and the retaining of records in the countries in which the user accesses the service; encouragement of ISPs to report information in child sexual exploitation; support for hotlines/tiplines and for their cooperation with law enforcement authorities; cooperation between national hotlines to develop an international database of information and best practices; development of a theoretical framework to support the rights of children to protection on the Internet; development and dissemination of 'net smart rules for kids'; awareness-raising among politicians, legislators, the media and civil society; criminalization of the production, distribution and possession of child pornography, including pseudo-pornography, research on the problem of anonymity on the Internet and framing of solutions; an intergovernmental conference on the protection of children against sexual exploitation on the Internet; the drafting of model legislation on child pornography, and design of software to check UseNet servers and delete child pornography.

> A partnership approach, characterized by a willingness to see all issues as common problems and supported by Government and the service provider industry, is the best way forward at this point in time. From *Illegal and Harmful Use of the Internet*, Department of Justice, Equality and Law Reform, Dublin, July 1998.

The report of the Interpol/ECPAT Experts Meeting could be taken as the framework for addressing the specific problem of child pornography on the Internet. There are roles and tasks for NGOs, law enforcement personnel, legislators and policy-makers, and Internet Service Providers. The challenge is to find ways in which to implement the ideas arising from that meeting. These include the creation of a task force with expertise in the field of computer and software technology and Internet service provision, law enforcement and legislation. The role of the task force would be to: promote the establishment of multi-agency units in every country that would target the elimination of sexual exploitation of children via the Internet; create or propose a framework in which such units (or where they did not exist, law enforcement agencies) would consult each other; devise an international awareness-raising campaign to inform ISPs and law enforcement agencies of the issues; in cooperation with the software industry to promote the development of a monitoring system which would block child pornography on the Net; provide an advice service to ISPs and law enforcement agencies on the use of software technology and of ways in which they could cooperate to eliminate child pornography on the

Internet; seek the participation of software producers in the quest to eliminate child pornography on the Internet; analyse and find answers to the data protection and freedom of speech issues, and suggest ways in which a permanent independent body might be set up to continue the work of the task force.

Answering training needs

It was suggested that the Interpol Standing Working Party on Offences against Minors (SWP) should not only continue to compile and maintain a resource list of training courses and expertise, but should also actively promote the use of the resource. SWP should provide information and advice to those seeking possible sources of funding and should support applications for such funding.

Addressing the difficulties in monitoring child pornography on the Internet

A number of ISPs should be invited to develop standards for record-keeping and tracing, develop standards for reporting, and fund research into the identification and tracking of anonymous users of child pornography.

Hotlines

The Internet Hotline in Europe Forum should continue its work of building up a database on information on hotlines and on best practices in their operation, which would include cooperation with ISPs and law enforcement agencies.

> These protection issues are wide-ranging, technically and legally complex and are international in their dimensions. They pose special challenges to the international community, governments, industry, educators, parents and indeed, individual users of the Internet. New partnerships, new approaches and new levels of flexibility will be needed to ensure that our exploitation of the Internet incorporates safety measures specifically designed to ensure maximum protection for those who are vulnerable to its downside. From *Illegal and Harmful Use of the Internet*, Department of Justice, Equality and Law Reform, Dublin, July 1998.

NGOs awareness raising

The Net Smart House Rules devised by groups within ECPAT-Europe should be promoted and developed. Campaigns should promote the efforts of governments, NGOs, ISPs and intergovernmental agencies in combating the problem of child pornography on the Internet, and raise awareness of the dangers to children.

Towards a theoretical framework

A Task Group of NGOs and academics should develop a theoretical framework that supports the rights of children to be protected on the Net and deals with the competing rights issues of free speech for adults.

Ratings systems

The work of the Internet Content Rating Alliance should be supported and promoted, so that an internationally acceptable system of categorization can be elaborated and adopted.

Model legislation to criminalize child pornography

Model legislation should be devised, drafted and disseminated by the United Nations Centre on Crime Prevention and Criminal Justice so that states would have the opportunity of harmonizing their legislation to combat child pornography on the Internet.

The Committee on the Rights of the Child

This Committee, which is tasked with monitoring the implementation of the Convention on the Rights of the Child, should pay particular attention to the manner in which states are addressing the problem of child pornography when it is considering states' reports under Article 34 of the Convention.

PART THREE

WHERE DO WE GO FROM HERE?

We are poised on the eve of a new millennium and this should be for us all a new departure. Judge Andrée Ruffo, President of the International Bureau for Children's Rights.

Chapter 28

DECLARATION AND PLAN OF ACTION

On 18–19 January 1999 some 300 specialists in child care and child protection, Internet specialists and service providers, media practitioners, law enforcement agencies and government representatives met at UNESCO Headquarters in Paris to consider ways of combating child pornography and paedophilia on the Internet. The Universal Declaration of Human Rights and the United Nations Convention on the Rights of the Child form the basis of UNESCO's efforts in this domain. Taking account of work already done, the expert meeting prepared a plan of action and issued a declaration, both of which are reproduced below.

Declaration

The Internet provides a new world for curious children. It offers entertainment and a new avenue for education, information and communication. The Internet is a tool that opens a window of opportunities, but is as yet available only to a tiny minority of the world's children. Today only five per cent of children have access to the Internet and most of these live in the developed regions of the world. This information gap between have and have not countries must be closed.

As Internet use grows, so do the risks of children being exposed to inappropriate material, in particular, criminal activity by paedophiles and child pornographers. While the benefits of the Internet far outweigh its potential drawbacks, these dangers cannot be ignored. If left unanswered, they pose a threat to children and will become the object of resistance to future Internet use.

We believe that future use of the Internet will be determined by the next generation born into a digital society and beginning to think, work, play and learn in fundamentally different ways from their parents. In this period of transition, however, the use and development of digital technologies must take account of current social, cultural and democratic values.

Above all, we need to know more about what is available on the Internet, its accessibility, the nature of the content, how many and which people consume it. Not enough is known about the scale or extent of paedophile activities on the Internet or their consequences and impact on young people.

Child protection on the Internet is not a matter of censorship. Ensuring that children are protected from harmful and illegal material must not compromise fundamental liberties, such as freedom of expression and information and the right to privacy.

The fight against paedophilia and child pornography on the Internet requires a coalition of forces involving children, the industry, policy makers, educators and parents to ensure that users are aware of the potential dangers and have available to them the necessary means to combat these threats.

Action against illegal content needs industry cooperation to restrict its circulation and a fully functioning system of self-regulation aiming at a high level of protection, going hand-in-hand with effective law enforcement. Harmful content needs to be treated differently from that which is clearly illegal.

In this spirit, we have identified concrete measures which are needed in order to encourage an environment favourable to the development of a child-friendly Internet. The following Action Plan requires a strategic approach which is both global and inclusive, and carries with it the commitment of all the actors, in particular governments, to ensure a framework of coordination, financial resources and political support. We request the Director-General to bring this Declaration and Action Plan to the attention of the Member States of UNESCO, the National Commissions and the General Conference.

The Internet is a formidable tool for education and culture. But we must work to safeguard freedom of expression, as in Article 19 of the Universal Declaration of Human Rights. We must also work hard to protect our children, as we pledged in Article 34 of the United Nations Convention on the Rights of Children, and as evinced in the Agenda for Action of the 1996 Stockholm Meeting. Director-General of UNESCO, 1999

Plan of Action

While the Plan of Action is addressed primarily to UNESCO, it contains elements which must be taken up by all actors in the fight against child pornography and paedophilia on the Internet. Governments, international agencies, NGOs, the industry, educators, parents, law enforcement agencies and the media all have a role to play, but a special effort should be made to ensure that the voice of children is also heard in the elaboration of strategies to make the Internet safe. UNESCO's role in this joint effort should be primarily that of a catalyst.

1. Research, awareness and prevention

Within its field of competence, UNESCO has a specific role and responsibility for action. In particular, a clearing house should be established for the exchange of information and to promote cooperation among groups concerned with the rights of children.

UNESCO's educational, cultural and communication programmes should take up the issues raised at the January meeting and in particular should:

- sponsor and develop initiatives for the use of technical means to combat harmful content on the Internet, particularly through the use of filters and self-rating systems;
- promote existing screening tools to make children and adults aware of how to protect themselves; and
- sponsor information campaigns which raise public awareness of the harm done to those who have been sexually abused.

In addition UNESCO should:

- systematically design and support research programmes in partnership with research institutions, to obtain a clearer, comprehensive and more up-to-date understanding of the problem of child pornography and paedophilia on the Internet;
- disseminate information among researchers, and promote exchange of information among child care and child protection organizations, Internet service providers, web masters, police and judicial institutions, media practitioners, citizens' and civic organizations and other concerned groups;
- commission the preparation of a comprehensive glossary of terms concerning the Internet and its operations so that users and specialists can arrive at a common understanding of this valuable informational and networking facility;
- support and encourage national 'hotlines' and the creation of networks of 'hotlines' or an international 'electronic watchtower' to enable children to get immediate help;
- develop media and Internet education, information and awareness strategies to sensitize children, parents, teachers, educational institutions, social workers, the media and decision-makers;
- involve mothers' and parents' associations in this common effort and create a strategic world network of citizens and personalities, institutions and industry to combat child pornography and paedophilia on the Internet; and
- develop a common long-term strategy to create a child-friendly cultural climate and promote the idea of a virtual civil society.

2. Law and regulation

UNESCO's role regarding law and regulation should be developed according to the following framework :

1. *targeted regulation* in support of anti-child-pornography laws to combat even the simple possession of pornographic materials;
2. *self-regulation* as a response by the Internet industry, and ethical guidelines to encourage the industry's broader participation;
3. *co-regulation*, which implies that regulation with the backing of governments, NGOs, industry and civil society should also be possible.

UNESCO in cooperation with other agencies and persons should set up a task force or expert committee bringing together experiences from all sectors seeking to combat pornography and paedophilia on the Internet in order to protect children. This action-oriented body should consider the following issues:

Prevention: promote awareness of the need for the protection of children online among all actors concerned, and including in particular law-making bodies and law enforcement agencies.

Collecting information: collect legal information of all kinds related to child pornography online including industry definitions and terminology on children's rights, child pornography and sexual abuses of children.

Disseminating information: widely disseminate and publicize via the Internet the information collected on legal issues related to child pornography and paedophilia online, making use of international observatories or clearing houses.

Analysis: conduct studies on legal issues related to child pornography and paedophilia online.

Self-regulation:
- study the efficiency of self-regulation;
- promote industry and private sector initiatives to develop codes of ethics on child pornography online working in parallel with judiciary experts worldwide;
- study the role of the Internet Service Provider (ISP) related to how paedophile networks are used;
- promote dialogue among all actors, governments and ISPs concerned to balance soft-law efforts.

Law-making :
- promote legal harmonization and international cooperation between the legal profession and the police;
- study, among other legal issues, the relevance and feasibility of an international legal framework to protect children online under the auspices of UNESCO.

International cooperation and law enforcement:
- promote appropriate standards for law enforcement and international cooperation, in coordination with Internet Service Providers;
- work towards the development of international principles or standards to facilitate cross-border law enforcement.

UNESCO

Chapter 29

THE WORLD CITIZENS' MOVEMENT TO PROTECT INNOCENCE IN DANGER

Homayra Sellier

The Internet has become a powerful means of communication and exchange for education and culture, but also for those who seek to exploit and abuse children through pornography and paedophilia. Imagine the 'personal' delivery of child pornography to the computer screen in your home in nanoseconds, from any point in the world, available to you, your spouse, and your children of any age. You need only 'click' and there it is!

But let us keep things in perspective. Admittedly, there are only some fifty sites identified so far that reveal child pornography, torture of children and other forms of sadomasochism. But they are there. There are probably another hundred still lurking in virtual space and yet to be found or to get online. Even so,ut these few sites deal in several hundred gigabytes of trafficked, illegal images. Images of naked, tortured, sexually abused children, abused by adults. Even one image is enough, for behind every image is a real child who has suffered more than you or I can ever imagine.

What is worse is when paedophiles discuss their philosophy and way of life, baring publicly their adult-child sexual relationships and their view that such relationships should be 'normal', and 'freely discussed', so that sexuality can be expressed by any child of any age with any adult! Such a philosophy is sick, and runs diametrically counter to all the human and ethical values we cherish. It is perversion plain and simple, and is as easily available on Internet as is bread at the baker's.

These paedophile sites openly discuss adult-child sex relations and defend this philosophy with impunity. There are over 23,000 such sites world-wide and some 40,000 chat groups. Their managers advertise these sites openly; they can be found by any search engine, for they use simple titles such as 'free spirits', 'boy lovers', 'man-boy' – words you would not be likely to programme into your filters to shut them out.

The problem is world-wide, because the Internet has made paedophilia and child pornography world-wide commercial products. Even in regions where computers and the Internet have reached fewer than 5 per cent of homes, such as in Asia and parts of Central and Latin America, the Internet is used to track sex tourism operators and the movement of children from one country to another, to trade child pornography, and sometimes even to arrange meetings with other pornographers and paedophiles, the better to advance their common business. In other words the Internet has made it possible for paedophiles to 'hide in the open'.

Countries that do not yet have the Internet to any great extent are wondering at present how to avoid these problems, while encouraging their people to learn and take advantage of the many educational and cultural benefits of worldwide networking.

Aware of these problems, the former Director-General of UNESCO called a meeting at UNESCO Headquarters in Paris on 18 and 19 January 1999 on the subject of Sexual Abuse of Children, Child Pornography and Paedophilia on the Internet. Some 350 specialists in child care and child protection, Internet specialists and service providers, media practitioners, law enforcement agencies and government representatives were convened on that occasion. Taking account of work that had already been done, this expert meeting prepared a plan of action and issued a declaration.

Paper recommendations though, are not enough. They need a soul. They need bodies to work and implement the plan of action. They also need ordinary citizens who can sensitize opinions and mobilize people and resources. The Director General of UNESCO accordingly encouraged a group of concerned citizens to hammer out specific ways of implementing the Plan of Action proposed by the said meeting. He proposed the 'creation of an international coalition of personalities composed of leading citizens to support major actions against the misuse of the Internet and for the benefit of children'. This group then conceived the idea of a World Citizens' Movement to Protect Innocence in Danger. The Movement would have a small international committee, the main work being done by national action groups and NGOs enlisting the participation of lawyers, Internet specialists, child protection organizations, jurists, political leaders and personalities such as actors and sports personalities, whose words could persuade others to think along the same lines and support world-wide efforts to stop child pornography and paedophilia on-line.

My appointment as President of Innocence in Danger was duly endorsed and I was invited to organize national action groups in Argentina, Belgium, Brazil, France, Monaco, Switzerland, the United Kingdom and the United

States. This has been done, and we are now seeking to organize more action groups in the Balkans, Cambodia, Greece, India, Italy, the Philippines, South Africa, Spain, Sri Lanka and Thailand, and wherever else children are in need of protection.

The Movement's supporters include Their Royal Highnesses the Crown Princess Maria Teresa of Luxembourg, Princess Caroline of Hanover and Princess Chantal of Greece, Baroness Silvia Amelia de Waldner, Sir Peter Ustinov, Marisa Berenson, Jean-Michel Folon and Maison Chopard, Geneva.

Since January 1999, the Innocence in Danger Movement, with the support of UNESCO and in collaboration with several NGOs, has worked on the following:

- A helpline to children, putting them directly in touch with social assistants, psychologists, doctors and the police if need be;
- An electronic watchtower to provide a news and information page, links to all NGOs working in this field, and an archive of relevant documents.
- A work entitled *Breaking the Chains of Silence*, presenting all the themes discussed at the January Conference, presented in thematic order and simplified for general reading.
- Special handbooks for teachers, parents and children, in the form of frequently asked questions concerning paedophilia, child pornography, legislation and the workings of the Internet. In effect, this volume will serve as a glossary and will be published in English, French and other languages.
- A survey on legislation concerning child pornography and paedophilia on the Internet. This is being done in cooperation with NGOs and individuals working on similar projects, such as the European Child Forum, the International Bureau of Children's Rights, and selected law schools and institutes.
- We have received contributions in cash, and more frequently in the form of services: secretarial work, writing and editing, legal surveys, cartoon work, and Internet web designs.

In this work, no one can act alone. We must reach out to each other. In the words of Margaret Mead, 'Never doubt that a small group of thoughtful, committed citizens can change the world, indeed it's the only thing that ever has done so'.

UNESCO acknowledges with gratitude the contribution of 75,000 FF by Maison Chopard, Geneva, to the work of the World Citizens' Movement to Protect Innocence in Danger.

Chapter 30

EPILOGUE: THE CHILD IS A PERSON

Carlos A. Arnaldo

This final word is being written with the benefit of hindsight from the perspective of two years' endeavour to carry out the recommendations of the UNESCO 1999 Expert Meeting on Sexual Abuse of Children, Child Pornography and Paedophilia on the Internet, and the experiences of working with other child protection specialists in a field where demands are increasing and resources are scarce. This book represents the combined thinking and experience of over 200 child care and child protection specialists and organizations, 20 representatives of law enforcement agencies including Interpol and Scotland Yard, 60 representatives of Members States, 157 journalists, and teachers, students, lawyers and clinical psychiatrists. The broad participation of all these partners at the meeting and in this written record bears witness to the worldwide concern now felt regarding the issues of child abuse in all its forms. Newspapers, radio and television provide a regular flow of heart-breaking news of child abuse and convictions and acquittals, with occasional in-depth coverage, while the European Commission has launched a major programme to protect children in the media and on the Internet in cooperation with many of the partners whose papers are included here.

That meeting and the papers that were prepared for it, together with relevant passages from other texts, in particular the United Nations Convention on the Rights of the Child, and a report of the Irish Department of Justice, Equality and Law Reform entitled *Illegal and Harmful Use of the Internet*, have opened a number of doors:

- Appearing in the wake of the Stockholm International Conference on the Commercial and Sexual Exploitation of Children (Stockholm, 1996) and the Expert Meeting on Child Pornography on the Internet (Lyons, 1997), this book provides an initial 'mapping' of what has been achieved by the various partners in the protection of children, child care, legislation and children's rights, and educational programmes to help children surf safely on the Internet.

- Child protection specialists will see from this book that they are not alone in their work, and that there is a vast network of police, researchers, informaticians, psychologists and psychiatrists, media practitioners and journalists, statesmen, students and young professionals who are ready to cooperate in this endeavour and whose contribution is invaluable.

- People are becoming increasingly aware of other organizations and are cooperating more and more actively with them. National citizens' action groups are springing up under the banner of the World Citizens' Movement to Protect Innocence in Danger, as recommended by the experts at the UNESCO meeting. These are now active in Albania, Argentina, Asia Pacific (based in Australia), Belgium, Brazil, Bulgaria, Cameroon, Canada, Colombia, Costa Rica, France, Greece, Ireland, Italy, Luxembourg, Monaco, Switzerland, the United Kingdom and the United States of America. The movement also looks for support from such agencies as End Child Prostitution, Child Pornography and Trafficking of Children for Sexual Purposes (ECPAT) and its associations in Sri Lanka, Thailand and many other parts of the world. The appeal on the Internet for voluntary contributions in service and in kind continues to be heeded. Many have offered to help in the form of writing, editing, infographics, a speaker's guild, books and documentation.

- The problem is rather better understood today in terms of its medical and legal parameters and its social implications. Ordinary people have a clearer picture of the dangers that confront them. However, much remains to be done for the victims of sexual abuse who suffer not only in childhood, but also into late adulthood. While it is important to strengthen the law and its enforcement, it is equally urgent to recognize the need for medical and psychiatric treatment for both victim and offender, not to mention their re-integration into society. This may call for a long-term approach, as the deeper trauma of sexual abuse are not curable in the short term. The new mix of specialists including police, therapists, researchers and doctors has brought new insights and approaches. Forums have been held in Athens, Brussels, Buenos Aires, London, Monaco, Montreal, Nairobi, New Delhi, Rio de Janeiro, Paris, Rome, San Antonio (Texas) and Yaoundé, among other locations.

- There is also a new and enhanced understanding of the various aspects of the problem of child abuse. Firstly, people are increasingly aware of the sexual abuse of children in almost every part of the world and at all levels of society, whether it be in the bosom of the family or through the sale of children, human trafficking and child prostitution that are prevalent especially in the poorest countries and those in conflict or in transition where despair and destitution frequently override all respect for human ethics. And secondly, people are learning of the potential risk to children of surfing on the Internet, of viewing adult and child pornography, and of coming into direct contact with potential child molesters and predators via 'chat rooms'. Solving one or other aspect of these problems is not enough. A holistic approach is necessary. Although many programmes of action have to restrict their scope in order to concentrate their limited resources, they should remain aware of the larger picture and take it fully into account.

- Partners are more cognizant today of the need for cooperation in enforcing the law against child abuse, child pornography and molestation by paedophiles. The International Bureau for Children's Rights (Montreal) has been influential in securing cooperation among twenty-two countries on entering into cross-border agreements for extradition and extra-territoriality. The Bureau has published an excellent comprehensive report in English and French on extraterritorial legislation and the three tribunals on child abuse that have been held in Brazil, France and Sri Lanka entitled *Global Report: International Dimensions of Sexual Exploitation of Children* (Montreal, International Bureau for Children's Rights, 1999).

- Many have urged the creation of a worldwide 'electronic watchtower' to collect and disseminate information, promote and support educational campaigns, and enable specialists to cooperate more dynamically and in every way they can. Research is viewed as a key factor in this respect, and in particular the regular compiling and presentation of research results for purposes of comparison and analysis. Three yearbooks on the protection of children have appeared, including *Children in the New Media Landscape: Games, Pornography, Perceptions* (Gothenburg, University of Gothenburg, International Clearing House on Children and Violence on the Screen, 2000). In a separate, related initiative, the Centre for the Study of Communication and Culture at St Louis University, Missouri, has devoted one of its quarterly reviews to the subject of 'Children and Television' (edited by Dr Norma Pecora, Ohio University, in *Communication Research Trends*, Vol. 19, Nos. 1 and 2, 1999, 61 pp.).

- Media fulfil a vital role in this field. They are society's watchdog, the voice of human conscience pointing out evil, praising success and providing reliable, objective information. Some news organizations have developed websites with search engines on issues such as child abuse and the conviction of child predators, and in-depth articles on ways to protect children in reality and online.

- Mediatized programmes also have an effective cultural and educational role to play, encouraging families, parents and teachers to guide their children in the use of all media, including the Internet. In this respect there is considerable scope for creativity in media education programmes, both in primary and secondary schools, and by reaching out directly to children on the web.
- The critical role of the specialized agencies of the United Nations system has been recognized. Each one has a contribution to make in its particular field, i.e. children's rights (United Nations Office of the High Commissioner for human rights), child labour (International Labour Organization), health and protection from AIDS (World Health Organization), sex tourism (World Tourism Organization), media education (UNESCO), and children in emergency situations (UNICEF).

The ultimate question is not whether the problem of child abuse can be solved once and for all through meetings or books or the media, or even through law enforcement or medicine: it is one of knowing why child abuse occurs, and whether through continuing research, juridical analysis, medical and psychiatric diagnosis, and even the study of cultural anthropology, we can gain a better grasp of the forces that motivate child sex offenders and so learn how to minimize the dangers hovering over the child.

What is it that urges certain adults to crash through the ethical barrier and surrender their children to abusers? Society has a duty to find the answer to such questions. Poverty or desperation cannot be the sole motive. Nor can it be simply the idea that the child is just a pawn in the family economy, or a cog of the consumer society, or a mere toy to be played with.

The child is a person.

ANNEXES

THE UNITED NATIONS CONVENTION ON THE RIGHTS OF THE CHILD

The States Parties to the present Convention,

Considering that, in accordance with the principles proclaimed in the Charter of the United Nations, recognition of the inherent dignity and of the equal and inalienable rights of all members of the human family is the foundation of freedom, justice and peace in the world,

Bearing in mind that the peoples of the United Nations have, in the Charter, reaffirmed their faith in fundamental human rights and in the dignity and worth of the human person, and have determined to promote social progress and better standards of life in larger freedom,

Recognizing that the United Nations has, in the Universal Declaration of Human Rights and in the International Covenants on Human Rights, proclaimed and agreed that everyone is entitled to all the rights and freedoms set forth therein, without distinction of any kind, such as race, colour, sex, language, religion, political or other opinion, national or social origin, property, birth or other status,

Recalling that, in the Universal Declaration of Human Rights, the United Nations has proclaimed that childhood is entitled to special care and assistance,

Convinced that the family, as the fundamental group of society and the natural environment for the growth and well-being of all its members and particularly children, should be afforded the necessary protection and assistance so that it can fully assume its responsibilities within the community,

Recognizing that the child, for the full and harmonious development of his or her personality, should grow up in a family environment, in an atmosphere of happiness, love and understanding,

Considering that the child should be fully prepared to live an individual life in society, and brought up in the spirit of the ideals proclaimed in the Charter of the United Nations, and in particular in the spirit of peace, dignity, tolerance, freedom, equality and solidarity,

Bearing in mind that the need to extend particular care to the child has been stated in the Geneva Declaration on the Rights of the Child of 1924 and in the Declaration of the Rights of the Child adopted by the General Assembly on 20 November 1959 and recognized in the Universal Declaration of Human Rights, in the International Covenant on Civil and Political Rights (in particular in articles 23 and 24), in the International Covenant on Economic, Social and Cultural Rights (in particular in article 10) and in the statutes and relevant instruments of specialized agencies and international organizations concerned with the welfare of children,

Bearing in mind that, as indicated in the Declaration of the Rights of the Child, the child, by reason of his physical and mental immaturity, needs special safeguards and care, including appropriate legal protection, before as well as after birth,

Recalling the provisions of the Declaration on Social and Legal Principles relating to the Protection and Welfare of Children, with Special Reference to Foster Placement and Adoption Nationally and Internationally; the United Nations Standard Minimum Rules for the Administration of Juvenile Justice (The Beijing Rules); and the Declaration on the Protection of Women and Children in Emergency and Armed Conflict,

Recognizing that, in all countries in the world, there are children living in exceptionally difficult conditions, and that such children need special consideration,

Taking due account of the importance of the traditions and cultural values of each people for the protection and harmonious development of the child,

Recognizing the importance of international co-operation for improving the living conditions of children in every country, in particular in the developing countries,

. . . have agreed as follows:

Part I

Article 1

For the purposes of the present Convention, a child means every human being below the age of 18 years unless, under the law applicable to the child, majority is attained earlier.

Article 2

1. States Parties shall respect and ensure the rights set forth in this Convention to each child within their jurisdiction without discrimination of any kind, irrespective of the child's or his or her parent's or legal guardian's race, colour, sex, language, religion, political or other opinion, national, ethnic or social origin, property, disability, birth or other status.
2. States Parties shall take all appropriate measures to ensure that the child is protected against all forms of discrimination or punishment on the basis of the status, activities, expressed opinions, or beliefs of the child's parents, legal guardians, or family members.

Article 3

1. In all actions concerning children, whether undertaken by public or private social welfare institutions, courts of law, administrative authorities or legislative bodies, the best interests of the child shall be a primary consideration.
2. States Parties undertake to ensure the child such protection and care as is necessary for his or her well-being, taking into account the rights and duties of his or her parents, legal guardians, or other individuals legally responsible for him or her, and, to this end, shall take all appropriate legislative and administrative measures.
3. States Parties shall ensure that the institutions, services and facilities responsible for the care or protection of children shall conform with the standards established by competent authorities, particularly in the areas of safety, health, in the number and suitability of their staff, as well as competent supervision.

Article 4

States Parties shall undertake all appropriate legislative, administrative, and other measures for the implementation of the rights recognized in the present Convention. With regard to economic, social and cultural rights, States Parties shall undertake such measures to the maximum extent of their available resources and, where needed, within the framework of international co-operation.

Article 5

States Parties shall respect the responsibilities, rights, and duties of parents or, where applicable, the members of the extended family or community as provided for by local custom, legal guardians or other persons legally responsible for the child, to provide, in a manner consistent with the evolving capacities of the child, appropriate direction and guidance in the exercise by the child of the rights recognized in the present Convention.

Article 6

1. States Parties recognize that every child has the inherent right to life.
2. States Parties shall ensure to the maximum extent possible the survival and development of the child.

Article 7

1. The child shall be registered immediately after birth and shall have the right from birth to a name, the right to acquire a nationality, and, as far as possible, the right to know and be cared for by his or her parents.
2. States Parties shall ensure the implementation of these rights in accordance with their national law and their obligations under the relevant international instruments in this field, in particular where the child would otherwise be stateless.

Article 8

1. States Parties undertake to respect the right of the child to preserve his or her identity, including nationality, name and family relations as recognized by law without unlawful interference.
2. Where a child is illegally deprived of some or all of the elements of his or her identity, States Parties shall provide appropriate assistance and protection, with a view to speedily re-establishing his or her identity.

Article 9

1. States Parties shall ensure that a child shall not be separated from his or her parents against their will, except when competent authorities subject to judicial review determine, in accordance with applicable law and procedures, that such separation is necessary for the best interests of the child. Such determination may be necessary in a particular case such as one involving abuse or neglect of the child by the parents, or one where the parents are living separately and a decision must be made as to the child's place of residence.
2. In any proceedings pursuant to paragraph 1, all interested parties shall be given an opportunity to participate in the proceedings and make their views known.
3. States Parties shall respect the right of the child who is separated from one or both parents to maintain personal relations and direct contact with both parents on a regular basis, except if it is contrary to the child's best interests.

4. Where such separation results from any action initiated by a State Party, such as the detention, imprisonment, exile, deportation or death (including death arising from any cause while the person is in the custody of the State) of one or both parents or of the child, that State Party shall, upon request, provide the parents, the child or, if appropriate, another member of the family with the essential information concerning the whereabouts of the absent member(s) of the family unless the provision of the information would be detrimental to the well-being of the child. States Parties shall further ensure that the submission of such a request shall of itself entail no adverse consequences for the person(s) concerned.

Article 10

1. In accordance with the obligation of States Parties under article 9, paragraph 1, applications by a child or his or her parents to enter or leave a State Party for the purpose of family reunification shall be dealt with by States Parties in a positive, humane and expeditious manner. States Parties shall further ensure that the submission of such a request shall entail no adverse consequences for the applicants and for the members of their family.
2. A child whose parents reside in different States shall have the right to maintain on a regular basis, save in exceptional circumstances personal relations and direct contacts with both parents. Towards that end and in accordance with the obligation of States Parties under article 9, paragraph 1, States Parties shall respect the right of the child and his or her parents to leave any country, including their own, and to enter their own country. The right to leave any country shall be subject only to such restrictions as are prescribed by law and which are necessary to protect the national security, public order (ordre public), public health or morals or the rights and freedoms of others and are consistent with the other rights recognized in the present Convention.

Article 11

1. States Parties shall take measures to combat the illicit transfer and non-return of children abroad.
2. To this end, States Parties shall promote the conclusion of bilateral or multilateral agreements or accession to existing agreements.

Article 12

1. States Parties shall assure to the child who is capable of forming his or her own views the right to express those views freely in all matters affecting the child, the views of the child being given due weight in accordance with the age and maturity of the child.
2. For this purpose, the child shall in particular be provided the opportunity to be heard in any judicial and administrative proceedings affecting

the child, either directly, or through a representative or an appropriate body, in a manner consistent with the procedural rules of national law.

Article 13

1. The child shall have the right to freedom of expression; this right shall include freedom to seek, receive and impart information and ideas of all kinds, regardless of frontiers, either orally, in writing or in print, in the form of art, or through any other media of the child's choice.
2. The exercise of this right may be subject to certain restrictions, but these shall only be such as are provided by law and are necessary:
   (a) For respect of the rights or reputations of others; or
   (b) For the protection of national security or of public order (ordre public), or of public health or morals.

Article 14

1. States Parties shall respect the right of the child to freedom of thought, conscience and religion.
2. States Parties shall respect the rights and duties of the parents and, when applicable, legal guardians, to provide direction to the child in the exercise of his or her right in a manner consistent with the evolving capacities of the child.
3. Freedom to manifest one's religion or beliefs may be subject only to such limitations as are prescribed by law and are necessary to protect public safety, order, health or morals, or the fundamental rights and freedoms of others.

Article 15

1. States Parties recognize the rights of the child to freedom of association and to freedom of peaceful assembly.
2. No restrictions may be placed on the exercise of these rights other than those imposed in conformity with the law and which are necessary in a democratic society in the interests of national security or public safety, public order (ordre public), the protection of public health or morals or the protection of the rights and freedoms of others.

Article 16

1. No child shall be subjected to arbitrary or unlawful interference with his or her privacy, family, home or correspondence, nor to unlawful attacks on his or her honour and reputation.
2. The child has the right to the protection of the law against such interference or attacks.

Article 17

States Parties recognize the important function performed by the mass media and shall ensure that the child has access to information and material from a diversity of national and international sources, especially those aimed at the promotion of his or her social, spiritual and moral well-being and physical and mental health. To this end, States Parties shall:

(a) Encourage the mass media to disseminate information and material of social and cultural benefit to the child and in accordance with the spirit of article 29;

(b) Encourage international co-operation in the production, exchange and dissemination of such information and material from a diversity of cultural, national and international sources;

(c) Encourage the production and dissemination of children's books;

(d) Encourage the mass media to have particular regard to the linguistic needs of the child who belongs to a minority group or who is indigenous;

(e) Encourage the development of appropriate guidelines for the protection of the child from information and material injurious to his or her well-being, bearing in mind the provisions of articles 13 and 18.

Article 18

1. States Parties shall use their best efforts to ensure recognition of the principle that both parents have common responsibilities for the upbringing and development of the child. Parents or, as the case may be, legal guardians, have the primary responsibility for the upbringing and development of the child. The best interests of the child will be their basic concern.

2. For the purpose of guaranteeing and promoting the rights set forth in the present Convention, States Parties shall render appropriate assistance to parents and legal guardians in the performance of their child-rearing responsibilities and shall ensure the development of institutions, facilities and services for the care of children.

3. States Parties shall take all appropriate measures to ensure that children of working parents have the right to benefit from child-care services and facilities for which they are eligible.

Article 19

1. States Parties shall take all appropriate legislative, administrative, social and educational measures to protect the child from all forms of physical or mental violence, injury or abuse, neglect or negligent treatment, maltreatment or exploitation including sexual abuse, while in the care of parent(s), legal guardian(s) or any other person who has the care of the child.

2. Such protective measures should, as appropriate, include effective procedures for the establishment of social programmes to provide necessary support for the child and for those who have the care of the child, as well

as for other forms of prevention and for identification, reporting, referral, investigation, treatment and follow-up of instances of child maltreatment described heretofore, and, as appropriate, for judicial involvement.

Article 20

1. A child temporarily or permanently deprived of his or her family environment, or in whose own best interests cannot be allowed to remain in that environment, shall be entitled to special protection and assistance provided by the State.
2. States Parties shall in accordance with their national laws ensure alternative care for such a child.
3. Such care could include, inter alia, foster placement, Kafala of Islamic law, adoption or if necessary placement in suitable institutions for the care of children. When considering solutions, due regard shall be paid to the desirability of continuity in a child's upbringing and to the child's ethnic, religious, cultural and linguistic background.

Article 21

States Parties that recognize and/or permit the system of adoption shall ensure that the best interests of the child shall be the paramount consideration and they shall:

(a) Ensure that the adoption of a child is authorized only by competent authorities who determine, in accordance with applicable law and procedures and on the basis of all pertinent and reliable information, that the adoption is permissible in view of the child's status concerning parents, relatives and legal guardians and that, if required, the persons concerned have given their informed consent to the adoption on the basis of such counselling as may be necessary;
(b) Recognize that inter-country adoption may be considered as an alternative means of child's care, if the child cannot be placed in a foster or an adoptive family or cannot in any suitable manner be cared for in the child's country of origin;
(c) Ensure that the child concerned by inter-country adoption enjoys safeguards and standards equivalent to those existing in the case of national adoption;
(d) Take all appropriate measures to ensure that, in inter-country adoption, the placement does not result in improper financial gain for those involved in it;
(e) Promote, where appropriate, the objectives of the present article by concluding bilateral or multilateral arrangements or agreements, and endeavour, within this framework, to ensure that the placement of the child in another country is carried out by competent authorities or organs.

Article 22

1. States Parties shall take appropriate measures to ensure that a child who is seeking refugee status or who is considered a refugee in accordance with applicable international or domestic law and procedures shall, whether unaccompanied or accompanied by his or her parents or by any other person, receive appropriate protection and humanitarian assistance in the enjoyment of applicable rights set forth in the present Convention and in other international human rights or humanitarian instruments to which the said States are Parties.

2. For this purpose, States Parties shall provide, as they consider appropriate, co-operation in any efforts by the United Nations and other competent intergovernmental organizations or non-governmental organizations co-operating with the United Nations to protect and assist such a child and to trace the parents or other members of the family of any refugee child in order to obtain information necessary for reunification with his or her family. In cases where no parents or other members of the family can be found, the child shall be accorded the same protection as any other child permanently or temporarily deprived of his or her family environment for any reason, as set forth in the present Convention.

Article 23

1. States Parties recognize that a mentally or physically disabled child should enjoy a full and decent life, in conditions which ensure dignity, promote self-reliance, and facilitate the child's active participation in the community.

2. States Parties recognize the right of the disabled child to special care and shall encourage and ensure the extension, subject to available resources, to the eligible child and those responsible for his or her care, of assistance for which application is made and which is appropriate to the child's condition and to the circumstances of the parents or others caring for the child.

3. Recognizing the special needs of a disabled child, assistance extended in accordance with paragraph 2 of the present article shall be provided free of charge, whenever possible, taking into account the financial resources of the parents or others caring for the child, and shall be designed to ensure that the disabled child has effective access to and receives education, training, health care services, rehabilitation services, preparation for employment and recreation opportunities in a manner conducive to the child's achieving the fullest possible social integration and individual development, including his or her cultural and spiritual development.

4. States Parties shall promote, in the spirit of international co-operation the exchange of appropriate information in the field of preventive health care and of medical, psychological and functional treatment of disabled children, including dissemination of and access to information concern-

ing methods of rehabilitation, education and vocational services, with the aim of enabling States Parties to improve their capabilities and skills and to widen their experience in these areas. In this regard, particular account shall be taken of the needs of developing countries.

Article 24

1. States Parties recognize the right of the child to the enjoyment of the highest attainable standard of health and to facilities for the treatment of illness and rehabilitation of health. States Parties shall strive to ensure that no child is deprived of his or her right of access to such health care services.
2. States Parties shall pursue full implementation of this right and, in particular, shall take appropriate measures:
   (a) To diminish infant and child mortality;
   (b) To ensure the provision of necessary medical assistance and health care to all children with emphasis on the development of primary health care;
   (c) To combat disease and malnutrition including within the framework of primary health care, through, inter alia, the application of readily available technology and through the provision of adequate nutritious foods and clean drinking water, taking into consideration the dangers and risks of environmental pollution;
   (d) To ensure appropriate pre-natal and post-natal health care for mothers;
   (e) To ensure that all segments of society, in particular parents and children, are informed, have access to education and are supported in the use of basic knowledge of child health and nutrition, the advantages of breast-feeding, hygiene and environmental sanitation and the prevention of accidents;
   (f) To develop preventive health care, guidance for parents, and family planning education and services.
3. States Parties shall take all effective and appropriate measures with a view to abolishing traditional practices prejudicial to the health of children.
4. States Parties undertake to promote and encourage international co-operation with a view to achieving progressively the full realization of the right recognized in the present article. In this regard, particular account shall be taken of the needs of developing countries.

Article 25

States Parties recognize the right of a child who has been placed by the competent authorities for the purposes of care, protection or treatment of his or her physical or mental health, to a periodic review of the treatment provided to the child and all other circumstances relevant to his or her placement.

Article 26

1. States Parties shall recognize for every child the right to benefit from social security, including social insurance, and shall take the necessary measures to achieve the full realization of this right in accordance with their national law.
2. The benefits should, where appropriate, be granted, taking into account the resources and the circumstances of the child and persons having responsibility for the maintenance of the child, as well as any other consideration relevant to an application for benefits made by or on behalf of the child.

Article 27

1. States Parties recognize the right of every child to a standard of living adequate for the child's physical, mental, spiritual, moral and social development.
2. The parent(s) or others responsible for the child have the primary responsibility to secure, within their abilities and financial capacities, the conditions of living necessary for the child's development.
3. States Parties, in accordance with national conditions and within their means, shall take appropriate measures to assist parents and others responsible for the child to implement this right and shall in case of need provide material assistance and support programmes, particularly with regard to nutrition, clothing and housing.
4. States Parties shall take all appropriate measures to secure the recovery of maintenance for the child from the parents or other persons having financial responsibility for the child, both within the State Party and from abroad. In particular, where the person having financial responsibility for the child lives in a State different from that of the child, States Parties shall promote the accession to international agreements or the conclusion of such agreements, as well as the making of other appropriate arrangements.

Article 28

1. States Parties recognize the right of the child to education, and with a view to achieving this right progressively and on the basis of equal opportunity, they shall, in particular:
    (a) Make primary education compulsory and available free to all;
    (b) Encourage the development of different forms of secondary education, including general and vocational education, make them available and accessible to every child, and take appropriate measures such as the introduction of free education and offering financial assistance in case of need;
    (c) Make higher education accessible to all on the basis of capacity by every appropriate means;

d) Make educational and vocational information and guidance available and accessible to all children;

(e) Take measures to encourage regular attendance at schools and the reduction of drop-out rates.

2. States Parties shall take all appropriate measures to ensure that school discipline is administered in a manner consistent with the child's human dignity and in conformity with the present Convention.

3. States Parties shall promote and encourage international co-operation in matters relating to education, in particular with a view to contributing to the elimination of ignorance and illiteracy throughout the world and facilitating access to scientific and technical knowledge and modern teaching methods. In this regard, particular account shall be taken of the needs of developing countries.

Article 29

1. States Parties agree that the education of the child shall be directed to:

(a) The development of the child's personality, talents and mental and physical abilities to their fullest potential;

(b) The development of respect for human rights and fundamental freedoms, and for the principles enshrined in the Charter of the United Nations;

(c) The development of respect for the child's parents, his or her own cultural identity, language and values, for the national values of the country in which the child is living, the country from which he or she may originate, and for civilizations different from his or her own;

(d) The preparation of the child for responsible life in a free society, in the spirit of understanding, peace, tolerance, equality of sexes, and friendship among all peoples, ethnic, national and religious groups and persons of indigenous origin;

(e) The development of respect for the natural environment.

2. No part of the present article or article 28 shall be construed so as to interfere with the liberty of individuals and bodies to establish and direct educational institutions, subject always to the observance of the principles set forth in paragraph 1 of the present article and to the requirements that the education given in such institutions shall conform to such minimum standards as may be laid down by the State.

Article 30

In those States in which ethnic, religious or linguistic minorities or persons of indigenous origin exist, a child belonging to such a minority or who is indigenous shall not be denied the right, in community with other members of his or her group, to enjoy his or her own culture, to profess and practise his or her own religion, or to use his or her own language.

Article 31

1. States Parties recognize the right of the child to rest and leisure, to engage in play and recreational activities appropriate to the age of the child and to participate freely in cultural life and the arts.
2. States Parties shall respect and promote the right of the child to fully participate in cultural and artistic life and shall encourage the provision of appropriate and equal opportunities for cultural, artistic, recreational and leisure activity.

Article 32

1. State Parties recognize the right of the child to be protected from economic exploitation and from performing any work that is likely to be hazardous or to interfere with the child's education, or to be harmful to the child's health or physical, mental, spiritual, moral or social development.
2. States Parties shall take legislative, administrative, social and educational measures to ensure the implementation of the present article. To this end, and having regard to the relevant provisions of other international instruments, States Parties shall in particular:
   (a) Provide for a minimum age or minimum ages for admission to employment;
   (b) Provide for appropriate regulation of the hours and conditions of employment;
   (c) Provide for appropriate penalties or other sanctions to ensure the effective enforcement of the present article.

Article 33

States Parties shall take all appropriate measures, including legislative, administrative, social and educational measures, to protect children from the illicit use of narcotic drugs and psychotropic substances as defined in the relevant international treaties, and to prevent the use of children in the illicit production and trafficking of such substances.

Article 34

States Parties undertake to protect the child from all forms of sexual exploitation and sexual abuse. For these purposes, States Parties shall in particular take all appropriate national, bilateral and multilateral measures to prevent:
   (a) The inducement or coercion of a child to engage in any unlawful sexual activity;
   (b) The exploitative use of children in prostitution or other unlawful sexual practices;
   (c) The exploitative use of children in pornographic performances and materials.

Article 35

States Parties shall take all appropriate national, bilateral and multilateral measures to prevent the abduction of, the sale of or traffic in children for any purpose or in any form.

Article 36

States Parties shall protect the child against all other forms of exploitation prejudicial to any aspects of the child's welfare.

Article 37

States Parties shall ensure that:

(a) No child shall be subjected to torture or other cruel, inhuman or degrading treatment or punishment. Neither capital punishment nor life imprisonment without possibility of release shall be imposed for offences committed by persons below 18 years of age;

(b) No child shall be deprived of his or her liberty unlawfully or arbitrarily. The arrest, detention or imprisonment of a child shall be in conformity with the law and shall be used only as a measure of last resort and for the shortest appropriate period of time;

(c) Every child deprived of liberty shall be treated with humanity and respect for the inherent dignity of the human person, and in a manner which takes into account the needs of persons of his or her age. In particular, every child deprived of liberty shall be separated from adults unless it is considered in the child's best interest not to do so and shall have the right to maintain contact with his or her family through correspondence and visits, save in exceptional circumstances;

(d) Every child deprived of his or her liberty shall have the right to prompt access to legal and other appropriate assistance, as well as the right to challenge the legality of the deprivation of his or her liberty before a court or other competent, independent and impartial authority, and to a prompt decision on any such action.

Article 38

1. States Parties undertake to respect and to ensure respect for rules of international humanitarian law applicable to them in armed conflicts which are relevant to the child.

2. States Parties shall take all feasible measures to ensure that persons who have not attained the age of 15 years do not take a direct part in hostilities.

3. States Parties shall refrain from recruiting any person who has not attained the age of 15 years into their armed forces. In recruiting among those persons who have attained the age of 15 years but who have not attained the age of 18 years, States Parties shall endeavour to give priority to those who are oldest.

4. In accordance with their obligations under international humanitarian law to protect the civilian population in armed conflicts, States Parties shall take all feasible measures to ensure protection and care of children who are affected by an armed conflict.

Article 39

States Parties shall take all appropriate measures to promote physical and psychological recovery and social reintegration of a child victim of: any form of neglect, exploitation, or abuse; torture or any other form of cruel, inhuman or degrading treatment or punishment; or armed conflicts. Such recovery and reintegration shall take place in an environment which fosters the health, self-respect and dignity of the child.

Article 40

1. States Parties recognize the right of every child alleged as, accused of, or recognized as having infringed the penal law to be treated in a manner consistent with the promotion of the child's sense of dignity and worth, which reinforces the child's respect for the human rights and fundamental freedoms of others and which takes into account the child's age and the desirability of promoting the child's reintegration and the child's assuming a constructive role in society.
2. To this end, and having regard to the relevant provisions of international instruments, States Parties shall, in particular, ensure that:
   (a) No child shall be alleged as, be accused of, or recognized as having infringed the penal law by reason of acts or omissions that were not prohibited by national or international law at the time they were committed;
   (b) Every child alleged as or accused of having infringed the penal law has at least the following guarantees:
      (i) To be presumed innocent until proven guilty according to law;
      (ii) To be informed promptly and directly of the charges against him or her, and, if appropriate, through his or her parents or legal guardians, and to have legal or other appropriate assistance in the preparation and presentation of his or her defence;
      (iii) To have the matter determined without delay by a competent, independent and impartial authority or judicial body in a fair hearing according to law, in the presence of legal or other appropriate assistance and, unless it is considered not to be in the best interest of the child, in particular, taking into account his or her age or situation, his or her parents or legal guardians;
      (iv) Not to be compelled to give testimony or to confess guilt; to examine or have examined adverse witnesses and to obtain the

participation and examination of witnesses on his or her behalf under conditions of equality;

(v) If considered to have infringed the penal law, to have this decision and any measures imposed in consequence thereof reviewed by a higher competent, independent and impartial authority or judicial body according to law;

(vi) To have the free assistance of an interpreter if the child cannot understand or speak the language used;

(vii) To have his or her privacy fully respected at all stages of the proceedings.

3. States Parties shall seek to promote the establishment of laws, procedures, authorities and institutions specifically applicable to children alleged as, accused of, or recognized as having infringed the penal law, and in particular:

(a) The establishment of a minimum age below which children shall be presumed not to have the capacity to infringe the penal law;

(b) Whenever appropriate and desirable, measures for dealing with such children without resorting to judicial proceedings, providing that human rights and legal safeguards are fully respected.

4. A variety of dispositions, such as care, guidance and supervision orders; counselling; probation; foster care; education and vocational training programmes and other alternatives to institutional care shall be available to ensure that children are dealt with in a manner appropriate to their well-being being and proportionate both to their circumstances and the offence.

Article 41

Nothing in the present Convention shall affect any provisions which are more conducive to the realization of the rights of the child and which may be contained in:

(a) The law of a State Party; or

(b) International law in force for that State.

Part II Implementation and monitoring

Article 42

States Parties undertake to make the principles and provisions of the Convention widely known, by appropriate and active means to adults and children alike.

Article 43

1. For the purpose of examining the progress made by States Parties in achieving the realization of the obligations undertaken in the present

Convention, there shall be established a Committee on the Rights of the Child, which shall carry out the functions hereinafter provided.

2. The Committee shall consist of ten experts of high moral standing and recognized competence in the field covered by this Convention. the members of the Committee shall be elected by States Parties from among their nationals and shall serve in their personal capacity, consideration being given to equitable geographical distribution, as well as to the principal legal systems.

3. The members of the Committee shall be elected by secret ballot from a list of persons nominated by States Parties. Each State Party may nominate one person from among its own nationals.

4. The initial election to the Committee shall be held no later than six months after the date of the entry into force of the present Convention and thereafter every second year. At least four months before the date of each election, the Secretary-General of the United Nations shall address a letter to States Parties inviting them to submit their nominations within two months. The Secretary-General shall subsequently prepare a list in alphabetical order of all persons thus nominated, indicating States Parties which have nominated them, and shall submit it to the States Parties to the present Convention.

5. The elections shall be held at meetings of States Parties convened by the Secretary-General at United Nations Headquarters. At those meetings, for which two thirds of States Parties shall constitute a quorum, the persons elected to the Committee shall be those who obtain the largest number of votes and an absolute majority of the votes of the representatives of States Parties present and voting.

6. The members of the Committee shall be elected for a term of four years. They shall be eligible for re-election if renominated. The term of five of the members elected at the first election shall expire at the end of two years; immediately after the first election, the names of these five members shall be chosen by lot by the Chairman of the meeting.

7. If a member of the Committee dies or resigns or declares that for any other cause he or she can no longer perform the duties of the Committee, the State Party which nominated the member shall appoint another expert from among its nationals to serve for the remainder of the term, subject to the approval of the Committee.

8. The Committee shall establish its own rules of procedure.

9. The Committee shall elect its officers for a period of two years.

10. The meetings of the Committee shall normally be held at United Nations Headquarters or at any other convenient place as determined by the Committee. The Committee shall normally meet annually. The duration of the meetings of the Committee shall be determined, and reviewed, if necessary, by a meeting of the States Parties to the present Convention, subject to the approval of the General Assembly.

11. The Secretary-General of the United Nations shall provide the necessary staff and facilities for the effective performance of the functions of the Committee under the present Convention.

12. With the approval of the General Assembly, the members of the Committee established under the present Convention shall receive emoluments from the United Nations resources on such terms and conditions as the Assembly may decide.

Article 44

1. States Parties undertake to submit to the Committee, through the Secretary-General of the United Nations, reports on the measures they have adopted which give effect to the rights recognized herein and on the progress made on the enjoyment of those rights:
   (a) Within two years of the entry into force of the Convention for the State Party concerned;
   (b) Thereafter every five years.

2. Reports made under the present article shall indicate factors and difficulties, if any, affecting the degree of fulfilment of the obligations under the present Convention. Reports shall also contain sufficient information to provide the Committee with a comprehensive understanding of the implementation of the Convention in the country concerned.

3. A State Party which has submitted a comprehensive initial report to the Committee need not, in its subsequent report submitted in accordance with paragraph 1 (b) of the present article, repeat basic information previously provided.

4. The Committee may request from States Parties further information relevant to the implementation of the Convention.

5. The Committee shall submit to the General Assembly of the United Nations through the Economic and Social Council, every two years, reports on its activities.

6. States Parties shall make their reports widely available to the public in their own countries.

Article 45

In order to foster the effective implementation of the Convention and to encourage international co-operation in the field covered by the Convention:

(a) The specialized agencies, the United Nations Children's Fund, and other United Nations organs shall be entitled to be represented at the consideration of the implementation of such provisions of the present Convention as fall within the scope of their mandate. The Committee may invite the specialized agencies, the United Nations Children's Fund and other competent bodies as it may consider appropriate to provide expert advice on the implementation of the Convention in areas falling within the scope of their respective mandates. The Committee may invite the specialized agencies, the United Nations Children's Fund, and other United Nations organs to submit reports on the implementation of the Convention in areas falling within the scope of their activities;

(b) The Committee shall transmit, as it may consider appropriate, to the specialized agencies, the United Nations Children's Fund and other competent bodies, any reports from States Parties that contain a request, or indicate a need, for technical advice or assistance along with the Committee's observations and suggestions, if any, on these requests or indications;

(c) The Committee may recommend to the General Assembly to request the Secretary-General to undertake on its behalf studies on specific issues relating to the rights of the child;

(d) The Committee may make suggestions and general recommendations based on information received pursuant to articles 44 and 45 of the present Convention. Such suggestions and general recommendations shall be transmitted to any State Party concerned and reported to the General Assembly, together with comments, if any, from States Parties

Part III

Article 46

The present Convention shall be open for signature by all States.

Article 47

The present Convention is subject to ratification. Instruments of ratification shall be deposited with the Secretary-General of the United Nations.

Article 48

The present Convention shall remain open for accession by any State. The instruments of accession shall be deposited with the Secretary-General of the United Nations.

Article 49

1. The present Convention shall enter into force on the thirtieth day following the date of deposit with the Secretary-General of the United Nations of the twentieth instrument of ratification or accession.

2. For each State ratifying or acceding to the Convention after the deposit of the twentieth instrument of ratification or accession, the Convention shall enter into force on the thirtieth day after the deposit by such State of its instrument of ratification or accession.

Article 50

1. Any State Party may propose an amendment and file it with the Secretary-General of the United Nations. The Secretary-General shall thereupon communicate the proposed amendment to States Parties, with a request that they indicate whether they favour a conference of States Parties for the purpose of considering and voting upon the proposals. In the event that, within four months from the date of such communication, at least one third of the States Parties favour such a conference, the Secretary-General shall convene the conference under the auspices of the United Nations. Any amendment adopted by a majority of States Parties present and voting at the conference shall be submitted to the General Assembly for approval.

2. An amendment adopted in accordance with paragraph 1 of the present article shall enter into force when it has been approved by the General Assembly of the United Nations and accepted by a two-thirds majority of States Parties.

3. When an amendment enters into force, it shall be binding on those States Parties which have accepted it, other States Parties still being bound by the provisions of the present Convention and any earlier amendments which they have accepted.

Article 51

1. The Secretary-General of the United Nations shall receive and circulate to all States the text of reservations made by States at the time of ratification or accession.

2. A reservation incompatible with the object and purpose of the present Convention shall not be permitted.

3. Reservations may be withdrawn at any time by notification to that effect addressed to the Secretary-General of the United Nations, who shall then inform all States. Such notification shall take effect on the date on which it is received by the Secretary-General.

Article 52

A State Party may denounce the present Convention by written notification to the Secretary-General of the United Nations. Denunciation becomes effective one year after the date of receipt of the notification by the Secretary-General.

Article 53

The Secretary-General of the United Nations is designated as the depositary of the present Convention.

Article 54

The original of the present Convention, of which the Arabic, Chinese, English, French, Russian and Spanish texts are equally authentic, shall be deposited with the Secretary-General of the United Nations.

In witness thereof the undersigned plenipotentiaries, being duly authorized thereto by their respective Governments, have signed the present Convention.

Adopted by the United Nations General Assembly 20 November 1989

LIST OF SITES FOR THE PROTECTION OF CHILDREN

At the request of very many persons and non-governmental organizations, this list of sites has been drawn up with the advice and counsel of a number of specialists. It is neither exhaustive nor exclusive, and should be monitored and updated regularly. Nor does it contain any sites that are *per se* commercial or have commercial announcements or teleshopping facilities within their pages. It is intended as a first set of principal references for children, their parents and teachers, and child protection specialists and institutions, to learn more about the operations of the Internet and such issues of concern as privacy, confidentiality, legal matters, filtering techniques, safety tips and specifically what other organizations and agencies are doing in this field.

UNESCO sites

Innocence in Danger

This site presents the follow-up action to the Experts' Meeting on Sexual Abuse of Children, Child Pornography and Paedophilia on the Internet. It explains the World Citizens' Movement to Protect Innocence in Danger and recaps key actions taken. The site also provides documents, audiovisual resources and kits for conducting information and teaching campaigns at country and in-country levels.

Website: http://www.unesco.org/webworld/innocence

Children's House

This is an interactive resource centre and a meeting place for the exchange of information that serves the well-being of children. It is a cooperative initiative of AIFS, the Children's Rights Centre, Childwatch, the Consultative Group on Early Childhood Care and Development, Child Rights International Network, Family Life Development Centre, IIN, NOSEB, Rädda Barnen, International Save the Children Alliance (ISCA), UNESCO, the World Bank and WHO. These various organizations create and manage the pages of this website that fall under their scope and mandate. Dedicated to supporting the generation and dissemination of knowledge about children's issues, *Children's House* facilitates the translation of the benefits of research and programming into policy and practice. The most important criteria for placing information in the *House* are the needs and concerns of children. Any specific institutional interests or promotion are generally more appropriately placed within individual web sites.
Website: http://childhouse.uio.no/index.html

UNESCO Observatory on the Information Society

The *Observatory*'s main objectives are to raise awareness on the constant evolution of ethical, legal and societal challenges brought about by new technologies. It aims to become a public service readily accessible to all by 1) providing updated information on the evolution of the Information Society at the national and international levels, and 2) fostering debates on related issues.
Website: http://www.unesco.org/webworld/observatory/index.html

UNESCO: INFO-ethics

Under the comprehensive theme of ethical, legal and societal Challenges of Cyberspace, this site presents The Second International Congress on Ethical, Legal and Societal Challenges of Cyberspace which was organized from 1-3 October 1998 in Monte Carlo, Monaco. Experts in telecommunication, information, computer science, social sciences and philosophy discussed the areas of public domain and multilingualism in cyberspace, privacy, confidentiality and security in cyberspace as well as societies and globalization. From this site one can also access the first INFO-ethics Conference held in Monaco in 1997.
Website: http://www.unesco.org/webworld/infoethics_2/index.htm

Other UN Specialized Agencies

The United Nations Children's Fund (UNICEF)

UNICEF advocates the protection of children's rights to meet their basic needs and expand their opportunities to reach their full potential. It helps developing countries build their capacity to form appropriate policies and deliver services for children and their families. UNICEF is committed to ensuring special protection for the most disadvantaged children — victims

of war, disasters, extreme poverty, all forms of violence and exploitation, and those with disabilities.
Website: http://www.unicef.org

The International Labour Organization

ILO formulates international labour standards in the form of conventions and recommendations, setting minimum standards of basic labour rights, such as freedom of association and the abolition of forced labour. The ILO is concerned about the rights of the child and child labour. The ILO is deeply involved in combating child prostitution as a labour problem.
Website: http://www.ilo.org

International organizations

Child Rights Information Network

CRIN is engaged in promoting international reflection on the ethical, legal and social issues of cyberspace and the Internet, and reducing violence on the screen. This site contains a wide range of information, news and links.
Website: http://www.crin.ch

Childnet International

This NGO networks with child welfare and educational groups, governments and international agencies to provide information on how children can benefit from, and be protected in using, international communications systems such as the Internet. 'On this site you can find out how we are developing projects which promote the new media to children and widen access to those who are marginalized, as well as see how we are working at the strategic level on initiatives which protect children in the use of new technologies.'
Website: http://www.childnet-int.org

Children@Risk

At the first World Congress Against Commercial Sexual Exploitation of Children, held in Stockholm in August 1996, Redd Barna (Save The Children, Norway), in cooperation with the Norwegian Ombudsman for Children, presented the international initiative 'children@risk' to fight child pornography on the Internet, being a campaign site against child pornography on the Internet, produced by Redd Barna, the Norwegian Section of International Save the Children Alliance.
Website: http://childhouse.uio.no/workshops

Defence for Children international (DCI)

DCI is an independent non-governmental organization set up during the International Year of the Child (1979) to ensure on-going, practical, systematic and concerted international action specially directed towards promoting and protecting the rights of the child. The organization's aims are: to foster awareness of, and solidarity around, children's rights situations, issues and initiatives throughout the world; to seek, promote and implement the most effective means of securing the protection of the rights in concrete situations, from both a preventive and a curative standpoint. DCI has consultative status with the United Nations Economic and Social Council, with UNICEF, UNESCO and the Council of Europe.

Website: http://www.childhub.ch/webpub/dcihome

ECPAT International (End Child Prostitution, Child Pornography and Trafficking of Children for Sexual Purposes)

ECPAT works on political action, law-making and law enforcement, awareness-raising in the tourist industry, education and media coverage. ECPAT started as a campaign against child prostitution in Asian tourism, but since the World Congress against Commercial Sexual Exploitation of Children, it has been combating commercial sexual exploitation of children on a worldwide basis. ECPAT has national groups and affiliates in 50 countries. A clippings service is available on the website.

Website: http://www.ecpat.net

The International Bureau of Children's Rights

The International Bureau deals with juridical process and extraterritorial legislation in response to the international dimension of child sexual exploitation. It has held children's tribunals in France (1997), Brazil (1998) and Sri Lanka (1999). The published report of the three tribunals became available in September 1999.

Website :   http://www.web.net/~tribunal

International Clearing House on Children and Violence on the Screen, Nordicom Documentation Centre, University of Gothenberg

The Clearing House, supported by the government of Sweden and UNESCO, collects and disseminates information on children, young people and media violence, seen from the perspective of the UN Convention on the Rights of the Child. It seeks to inform various groups of users — researchers, policy-makers, media professionals, teachers, voluntary organizations and interested individuals — about research findings concerning children, young people and media violence; ongoing research on children and media violence; children's access to mass media and their media use; training and courses of study on children and the media; positive alternatives to media violence; and measures and activities which aim to limit gratuitous violence on television, in films and in interactive media. Two yearbooks were published in 1998 and 1999. The yearbook for 2000 is planned to be on the issue of pornography in the media and on the Internet.

Website: http://www.nordicom.gu.se/unesco.html

The International Save The Children Alliance (ISCA)

ISCA coordinates activities that encompass development assistance for, and advocacy of, children's rights, and is extended through the work of its 25 members in over 100 countries throughout the world.
Website: http://www.savechildren.or.jp/alliance

International Society for the Prevention of Child Abuse and Neglect (ISPCAN)

ISPCAN's mission is to prevent cruelty to children in every nation, in whatever form: physical abuse, sexual abuse, neglect, street children, child prostitution.
Website: http://www.ispcan.org

The Internet Watch Foundation

IWF is an independent industry watchdog. By March 1999, it had removed almost 2,000 images of child sex from the internet.
Website: http ://www.iwf.org.uk

Interpol

One may wonder why Interpol is involved with the investigation of crime against children. Why should a criminal police organization concern itself with children as victims of crime? Interpol provides information on the web about children, possible abuses, and what the international police organization can do to detect crimes and track down criminals. Adults who victimize children are actually the worst offenders.
Website: http ://www.interpol.int/public/children/default.asp

Movement Against Paedophilia on the Internet (MAPI)

MAPI is a research group working on paedophilia and child pornography on the Internet. MAPI's objectives are to promote interdisciplinary research in the field, inform users of the Internet and be available for Internet Providers concerning advice and recommendations.

http://www.info.fundp.ac.be/~mapi/plan.html will show the complete MAPI report on paedophilia on the Internet.
Website: http://www.info.fundp.ac.be/~mapi/mapi-fr.html

The Focal Point Against Sexual Exploitation of Children

This is the programme of the NGO group for the Convention on the Rights of the Child (CRC). It was created to facilitate exchanges and collaborative activities among a broad Support Group made up of IGOs, NGOs and individual experts and plays a leading role in monitoring at international level the issues of sexual exploitation, abuse and violence where children and youth are victims. The group dealing with these issues has contributed to the development of the relevant articles of the Convention dealing with the subject and to the drafting of a UN Programme of Action on the Sale of Children, Child Prostitution and Child Pornography. It participates in dis-

cussions dealing with a draft optional protocol to the CRC on the same issues. It has made an input in the preparation of the new ILO Convention on the worst forms of child labour which covers trafficking, child prostitution and child pornography. This site provides background information, policy papers on these themes, research and studies that can be downloaded, and a regular newsletter including a calendar of events.
Website: www.childhub.ch/dcifp/focalpoint.html

Redd Barna

The Norwegian Office of Save the Children, is an international organization that handles all major activities in favour of children. This work includes referring child pornography cases to the Norwegian Police and seeing that each case is handled by the appropriate national or international agency.
Website for Norway: http://childhouse.uio.no/redd_barna

For Sweden – which also contains material about the World Congress against Commercial Sexual Exploitation of Children, which took place in Stockholm, Sweden, in 1996:   http://www.rb.se/engindex.htm

World Congress against Commercial Sexual Exploitation of Children

Site provides the report, action plan, papers and press materials, and several fact sheets of this first world congress.
Website: http://www.childhub.ch/webpub/csechome

Regional and National Organizations

These sites are placed here as regional organizations, though the global operations of the Internet have made many of them effectively 'international'. Even so-called national organizations have had to reach out internationally to work effectively, as the problems have also travelled across borders. They are nonetheless listed as regional or in some cases, national, since that is their principal outreach and vocation.

Ask Jeeves for Kids!

This site presents a method for children to ask questions in simple language, without the technicalities of logical query markers such as 'and', or 'not', of some search engines. Replies are often given in an interactive way that urges users to click and search for more information.
Website: http://www.ajkids.com

Australian National Child Protection Clearing House

This is a network of people and publications including newsletters, issues and discussion papers and bibliographies, a listing of organizations around the world and a searchable database of prevention programs.
Website: http://www.aifs.org.au/external/nch/nch_menu

Casa Alianza

This non-governmental organization is dedicated to the rehabilitation and defence of street children in Guatemala, Honduras and Mexico. Casa Alianza monitors and cares for about 3,000 street children, most of whom have been orphaned by civil war or abused or rejected by their families, and who as a result are begging, stealing or selling themselves for a hot meal, a shower, a clean bed. They have actively militated for justice even against threats to their own personnel. Casa Alianza has contributed to arranging for a two-week inspection visit of the UN Special Rapporteur to Guatemala.

Website: http://www.casa-alianza.org

Center for Media Education (CME)

CME is a national non-profit organization dedicated to improving the quality of electronic media, especially on behalf of children and families. Up-to-date information is provided on critical issues, particularly CME's suggestions to ensure effective rules to implement the Children's Online Privacy Protection Act.

Website: http://www.cme.org

Childnet International hotlines

Internet Hotline Providers in Europe (INHOPE) Forum is a project initially funded under the European Commission Daphne programme to bring together the main hotlines/tiplines in Europe that deal with child pornography and other illegal material on the Internet. The Forum is serviced by Childnet International.

Website: www.childnet-int.org/hotlines

The Forum plans to become a more formal Association and a new website will be available.

Website: www.inhope.org

Cyberangels

Cyberangels is a non-profit organization with the goal of educating parents, teachers and child Internet users on online safety. They also have teams of volunteers who search the Internet for child pornography and work with law enforcement agencies around the world to report paedophile luring activities online. They hold classes online to teach safety and have one of the most popular volunteer tiplines at the site to report cybercrimes against children.

Website: http://www.cyberangels.org

Cyberrights and Cyberliberties

This is an extensive site dealing with the regulation of child pornography on the Internet. Monitors mainly UK cases. Also many links to other sites dedicated to fighting child pornography on the internet.

Website: http://www.leeds.ac.uk/law/pgs/yaman/child.htm

Enough is Enough

This is an artistically and meaningfully well-executed site on safety tips for parents and children on the net. Navigation is simple.

Website: http://www.enough.org

Federal Bureau of Investigation

While online computer exploration opens a world of possibilities for children, expanding their horizons and exposing them to different cultures and ways of life, they can be exposed to dangers as they hit the road exploring the information highway. There are individuals who attempt to sexually exploit children through the use of online services and the Internet. Some of these individuals gradually seduce their targets by giving them attention, affection, kindness and even gifts. These individuals are often willing to devote considerable amounts of time, money and energy in this process. For this reason, the FBI has presented this pamphlet online to help surfers begin to understand the complexities of online child exploitation.

Website: http://www.fbi.gov/library/pguide/pguide.htm

Filtering Facts

This is a non-profit organization in the United States that works to protect children from the harmful effects of pornography by promoting the use of filtering software in libraries. It provides the information that citizens, librarians and activists need to counter misperception and misinformation about the prevalence of Internet pornography in libraries and the efficacy of filtering programs for European users. This was funded by the European Commission in 1999. The site contains information about their work and coming events, and provides documents and news reports.

Website: http://www.incore.org

News Agency for Children's Rights

ANDI is a non-governmental organization whose mission is to contribute to raising awareness, within the media, of the promotion and defence of children's and adolescents' rights, considering that the democratization of their access to basic social rights is a fundamental condition for social equity. Most items are in Portuguese.

Website: http:/www.andi.org.br

Eurochild

The mission of the Centre for Europe's Children is to provide information for policy-makers, academics and experts responsible for child-related activities. It is an important online resource for information on children in Europe and has a large section on Child Protection.
Website: http://eurochild.gla.ac.uk

The European Forum for Child Welfare

EFCW is a network of non-governmental organizations (NGOs) concerned with child welfare across Europe. EFCW is itself part of a wider network, the International Forum for Child Welfare. EFCW welcomes members from all European countries. To date, members come from 20 countries, including Central and Eastern Europe. The Forum aims to service its members and enable them to provide high quality practice for children throughout Europe. In addition, it aims to raise the profile of child welfare with the European Institutions. Texts in English and French.
Website: http://www.efcw.org/

National Center for Missing and Exploited Children

NCMEC spearheads national efforts in the United States to locate and recover missing children and raise public awareness about ways to prevent child abduction and molestation; portrays children's photographs, with one in seven of the children recovered as a direct result.
Website: http://www.missingkids.org

NCH Action for Children (United Kingdom)

This site seeks to improve the lives of Britain's most vulnerable children and young people by providing a diverse and innovative range of services for them and their families, and campaigning on their behalf. It includes guides for parents as well as information on various initiatives to provide a watch on the internet.
Website: http://www.nchafc.org.uk/home.html

A Parent's Guide to the Internet

This book is online for free. The author, Parry Aftab, is a cyberspace lawyer and child safety advocate. This site is devoted to teaching online safety to parents, children and teachers. Ms. Aftab has developed programmes to be taken into schools and teach parents and children about online safety and how paedophiles get past children's 'stranger danger' defenses. Her new book, *The Parents' Guide to Protecting Children in Cyberspace*, was published in October 1999 (McGraw-Hill) and the royalties earned will benefit child online safety programs.
Website: http://www.familyguidebook.com

PBS TechKnow

This site is generally a fun and games site for young children. It has a special page in interactive language to learn safety tips on the net in a 'fun' way.

Website: http://www.pbs.org/kids/fungames/techknow/

People's Recovery, Empowerment and Development Assistance Foundation

The PREDA Foundation is a small but proactive, charitable, not-for-profit organization working on a national and international level for Human Rights, especially Women's and Children's Rights. It runs a residential therapeutic community for abused and exploited children. PREDA campaigns against child labour, the sexual exploitation of children, and seeks to educate about Aids. There is a full archive for documentation, information and news campaigns. PREDA has also been instrumental in bringing in new legislation concerning conviction of paedophiles and child abusers.

Website: http://www.preda.org

Privacy Rights Clearinghouse

The PRC offers consumers a unique opportunity to learn how to protect their personal privacy. Publications provide in-depth information on a variety of informational privacy issues, as well as practical tips on safeguarding personal privacy. Numerous news items and fact sheets are issued regularly.

Website: http://www.privacyrights.org/fs/children.htm

Safe Use of the Internet

This website is part of a unique research project of the European Union, Pilot Awareness Project, to assess how best to encourage the safe use of the Internet by children across Europe.

Website: http://www.netaware.org

Safeguarding Our Children - United Mothers

SOC-UM, as it is better known, is a non-profit organization dedicated to public awareness, education and prevention of child abuse. SOC-UM also serves as a resource to those who have been wounded by childhood abuse. The site is highly informative and interactive, and provides access to information both for safety tips as well for understanding the phenomena of child abuse and paedophilia. Additionally, it provides hotlines, ways of reporting illegal sites or information related to those subjects that pose a danger to children. SOCUM provides acknowledgement to cooperative organizations and sites fighting the same battle.

Website: http://www.soc-um.org

Safekids and Safeteens

These are two sites created and updated by Larry Magid, a columnist for the newspaper, the Los Angles *Times*, Internet writer and author of *The Little PC Book*. The sites offer articles, safety tips for kids and teens, as well as for their parents, references, academic and technical briefs as well as news articles, and well-selected links to other sites.

Website: http://ww.safekids.com
http://www.safeteens.com

Save the Children Alliance (ISCA)

Founded in London on 19 May 1919 by Eglantyne Jebb and her sister, Dorothy Buxton. Save the Children was the forerunner of the original International Save the Children Alliance in Geneva. Today, the Alliance's 25 member organizations support a wide variety of programme activities in over 100 countries. The current chair of the Alliance is Rädda Barnen (Save the Children, Sweden) and coordination is provided by a small secretariat in Geneva. All of our work is based on the rights of the child, first expressed by Save the Children's founder and now enshrined in the United Nations Convention on the Rights of the Child.

Website: http://www.savechildren.or.jp/alliance

The Three Little Cyberpigs

This site offers an animated computer game for children created by the Media Awareness Network, Canada. In their first adventure, *Privacy Playground*, the Cyberpigs learn to protect their personal privacy on the Internet. In *Cybersense* and *Nonsense* the Three Cyberpigs, Les, Mo and Lil, explore the world of online chat rooms. Cybersense and Nonsense is designed to help children between the ages of nine and twelve learn to distinguish between biased, prejudicial information and factual, objective information, and to detect bias and harmful stereotyping in online content. Players are introduced to an accepted online code of conduct ('netiquette'), and to the concept that information is not necessarily true just because it is on the Internet. The game is accompanied by an online Teachers Guide for use at home or in the classroom. The guide reviews the sequences in the game, gives background information on the issues of cyberhate and netiquette, and provides related pre- and post-game activities, along with printable student handouts. Site is in English or French.

Website: http://www.media-awareness.ca/eng/cpigs/cpigs2.htm

Wiredkids

This is a funsite that is interesting and helpful in providing Internet information for parents, kids, librarians and teachers. It was created by the United States National Action Committee of the World Citizens' Movement to Protect Innocence in Danger. It aims to provide links to resources around the world on on-line safety, equitable access and child advocacy issues. It has links to tiplines and helplines, and practical information about filtering, search engines, Internet access and online safety programs. Our Cybermoms program will prepare parents to teach online safety to other parents and to children in schools, community centres and libraries. The site also has downloadable worksheets and presentations for children and parents.

Website: www.wiredkids.org

Wired News

Wired News is a news service specializing in latest information on Internet, informatics and generally any subject that relates back to informatics and telematics.

Website: http://www.wired.com/news/news

Virlanie Foundation

Established in 1988, this organization works with street children and young prostitutes in Manila, Philippines, giving them shelter, food, education and love. Virlanie thus welcomes abandoned children, street beggars, young prostitutes, physically and emotionally battered children, mentally handicapped children and victims of incest. Site is presented in English and French.

Website: http://www.vasia.com/virlanie/indexf.htm

Yahooligans

This site, a youth-oriented version of the better known search engine, Yahoo!, provides simplified ways for young people to search sites on subjects of interest to them, notably sports, music entertainment, arts, science and nature, mathematics, computers and games.

Website: http://www.yahooligans.com

Young Media Australia

This site provides learning guides for parents, cybersafety tips, and is now available as part of a hands-on special pilot project called the Parents' Internet Resource Centre. It is funded by the Department of Communications and the Arts. The site provides easy introductions to basic concepts of the Internet and special courses for parents.

Website: http://www.youngmedia.org.au/yma/cyber.html

INDEX